Never Enough:

Lessons from a Recovering Workaholic

Never Enough:

Lessons from a Recovering

Workaholic

Dr. Frank O'Neill

Foreword by Dr. Joseph J. Sweere

iUniverse, Inc.
New York Bloomington

iUniverse books may be ordered through booksellers or by contacting:

iUniverse
1663 Liberty Drive
Bloomington, IN 47403
www.iuniverse.com
1-800-Authors (1-800-288-4677)

Because of the dynamic nature of the Internet, any Web addresses or links contained in this book may have changed since publication and may no longer be valid. The views expressed in this work are solely those of the author and do not necessarily reflect the views of the publisher, and the publisher hereby disclaims any responsibility for them.

ISBN: 978-1-4502-0373-9 (sc)
ISBN: 978-1-4502-0381-4 (hc)
ISBN: 978-1-4502-0379-1 (ebook)

Library of Congress Control Number: 2010900812

Printed in the United States of America

iUniverse rev. date: 01/18/10

This book is dedicated to everyone
who is trying to make this world a better place.

Acknowledgments

To mom and dad, thank you for believing in me when I did not. I love you more than you will ever know. Not a day goes by that you are not in my heart. Your love and support have transformed my life.

To Jack, Rick, and Tanner, thank you for bringing so much laughter, joy, and love into my life. We have developed bonds that nothing could ever break. Each of you has a special place in my heart.

To my Lord and Savior, thank you for the strength to do what is right in a world that does not always reward you for those actions. You constantly remind me that there is no right way to do the wrong thing. Thank you for teaching me the joy of helping my fellow man.

To anyone who has ever wronged me, thank you. The life lessons that I have learned along the way have made me the man that I am today.

Finally, to anyone that is hurting, never give up hope. Over 150,000 people died yesterday, and you were not one of them. That is a start.

Table of Contents

Foreword

After many years of dedicated study, personal sacrifice, and economic deprivation, it is understandable how young people can get caught up in the relentless chase after the Great American Dream—only to find their lives becoming tangled in a living nightmare. This book provides the reader with an honest appraisal of the material temptations that commonly befall this generation as they join the professional community. From heart rending to hilarious, Dr, O'Neill's story is one of choices made and lessons learned. The message is richly woven with time-honored wisdom that led him back to redemption and renewal. His message will serve as a guide for those who may be feeling the flames of burnout snatching at their heels.

Each chapter shines with deep pearls of insight and practicality. Dr. O'Neill helps us understand that soul-searching in every aspect of our life journey is the key to restoring the fabric of a torn and damaged spirit. His words serve as sound counsel in realizing the desired outcome of achieving a state of balance that harmonizes our life experience. The critical factors he identifies include our chosen career, family, social life, finances, personal health, emotional state, time management, and attunement with our inner spirit.

Of primary importance within the workaholic prevention and recovery model that Dr. O'Neill provides is an ability to recognize and manage stress in our daily experiences. He outlines a simple, seven-point formula that includes journaling, laughter, engaging hobbies, physical exercise, quiet time, conversation and prayer, all cradled in an atmosphere of optimism and positive expectancy. He also discusses a list of what-not-to-do's, such as television addiction, for example, which robs viewers of adequate sleep and instead too often programs our psyche with thousands of hours of mind-numbing superficiality, off-color sexual innuendo and non-stop violence.

You'll relish the time-honored and sage wisdom of the many quotes he has chosen to enhance his message and the Life Lessons he uses to summarize each chapter.

Optimal health has been defined as a manifestation of harmony within the body, mind and spirit. The renowned Lebanese philosopher Kahlil Gibran suggests that work is love made visible. You may decide to ask yourself this simple question: Does my work provide the same level of satisfaction and joy in my own life as it does for those whom I serve? If pursuing your American Dream is keeping you from sleeping soundly, this book is a must-read. Its message clearly reminds us that the best things in life are not things, that human needs are more than physical, and what matters most is not material.

Thank you Dr. O'Neill. The world needs more of the likes of you!

Dr. Joseph J. Sweere – Professor, Department of Clinical Sciences, Northwestern Health Sciences University, and author of *Golden Rules for Vibrant Health in Body, Mind, and Spirit*

Introduction

Old Habits Die Hard

August 10, 2007, is a day that I hate to remember and I cannot afford to forget. It was the day that my life ended as I knew it. On August 9th, I was the owner of three chiropractic clinics, the team doctor for three universities, a business consultant, and a researcher for a clinical study on pain management. Then it all came crashing down. I cracked under the pressure of my workaholic lifestyle, and I watched my career—and my future—land in the toilet.

I had done everything that my practice management consultants told me to do. I had done everything that my business partner expected me to do. I had neglected to do what I wanted to do. I had become a slave to my work, and I was tired, hurt, and mad.

When I was not busy seeing patients, I was doing paperwork or scrubbing toilets. I was working too much, but it was paying off. I built my business up much faster than expected, and the money started to roll in. Looking at it from the outside, I was a huge success. The only problem is that I was dying on the inside.

My relationships started to crumble. I started to take my frustration out on the people that I loved the most. I resented them for pulling me away from my career. Why did they not understand how hard I was working to make a better future for us all? I had promised myself that I would work tirelessly for two or three years, and then be able to slow down and coast. Two or three years quickly turned into six or seven. I had no idea that it took as much time and energy to maintain a successful career as it did to build one.

My body also failed me. I went from running six miles a day in 2003 to struggling to climb out of bed in the morning in 2006. I went from kayaking and cycling on the weekends in 2004 to spending my weekends on the couch with a bottle of Jim Beam in 2007. I was suffering from excruciating migraine headaches on a weekly basis. I had persistent heartburn, I was vomiting blood, and I was eating ibuprofen like candy just to get by. I was truly running on empty.

I never took the time that I needed to recharge my batteries, and it finally caught up with me. I had been working myself so hard for so many years that my body gave out. I felt like I had aged twenty years overnight. I had to face the fact that I was killing myself.

This brings us to that fateful day. I slumped into my office chair after a sixteen-hour day, wondering what I was doing with my life. No matter how much money I made, it could never be worth it. I would have a lot of money and nice things, but I wouldn't be healthy or happy enough to enjoy them. That realization finally brought me to my knees. It was me versus the superficial world that I had created, and the world had finally won. I quit the next day; I gave up. In 24 hours, I went from being a business success to an unemployed soul-searcher. I knew that I had to get out of the business world to save my life.

I quickly learned that I wasn't making my choices; my choices were making me. The path that I had chosen for my life brought me face-to-face with my inner demons. I let my career success get in the way of my personal life, and it got the best of me. I knew that the only way I was going to save myself was to change. I put everything else on hold to discover how. On August 10th, my focus switched from business success to physical, emotional, and spiritual recovery. I had to rethink every aspect of my life and make health and happiness my top priorities.

I knew that my journey back would be a long and difficult one. The key to my recovery began with the creation of a step-by-step plan for my life. I used the left side of my brain to create a system to get from where I was to where I wanted to be. I used the right side of my brain to develop creative solutions to the struggles that I encountered along the way. Then I took the first step towards a better me.

The journey transformed every aspect of my life, and my plan grew and developed into the book that you are holding. I used the information covered in these pages to create a passionate life that is truly my own. By picking up this book, you have taken the first step towards realizing these promises in your own life. And, I might add, not a moment too soon.

Statistically speaking, you will live for twenty-eight thousand days. These days will move on indifferently, constantly, at the same rate, regardless of whether you want them to pass quickly or last forever. Once a day has passed, it is gone. Most of us are wasting this precious time—barely surviving on a life support system of television and Prozac. We may as well be in a coma. As Benjamin Franklin put it: "Most people die at age twenty-five, but they are not buried until age seventy-five." You cannot afford to postpone your life for another moment.

Our frenzied pace of life has caused us to consider a different path—to realize that it does not have to be this way. I refuse to believe that we are not meant for better days. The tips in this book will help you balance what you need to do and have to do with what you want to do, so that you can find the happiness that comes with the creation of a life worth living.

Answer the most important question first: Why did you pick up this book? You must be feeling that you have a personal destiny that is different from the life that you are living now. Perhaps you have that uneasy feeling in the pit of your stomach that signals a soul in distress. Some of the things that could be tugging at you to change include:

- Lost enthusiasm for your work
- The desire to be energized by something new
- Feeling burdened by your job
- The need to create a meaningful life
- The feeling that there has got to be something more

Every one of these points begged me for my attention. They posed questions that demanded an answer. The path of discovery that followed has taken me to the greatest point in my life. This leads me to my challenge to you. What better place than here? What better time than now? I was able to take my life back. What is stopping you?

If you do not do something with this information, there will always be that persistent feeling that you have missed an opportunity.

You will be forced to wonder if you could have done more with your life. If you try to make the right life for yourself, succeed or fail, you win. You win because you will have learned that you care enough about yourself to try. You will have also learned that you do not have to settle for a mediocre life. If you are going to go down, you should go down swinging.

Take it from me. I am the voice of painful experience. I lost my job, my health, my self-respect, and my sanity in a few short months. I hurt my family, my friends, and my patients to get ahead in life, and I may never completely forgive myself. I am an expert on this subject because I have screwed up so many times that I have learned what not to do. I just hope that you can learn from my mistakes without having to suffer the same consequences.

We are all creatures of habit, from our favorite sports teams to our favorite spot on the couch. That is why "new" Coke was such a flop. Research has shown that it takes twenty-one days to create a new habit. Read this book from cover to cover. Answer all of the questions that are asked of you. Then give yourself twenty-one days to...

"I get pretty impatient with people who are able-bodied, but are paralyzed for other reasons."

-Actor Christopher Reeve

Part I: Love Yourself

"That the birds of worry fly above your head, this you cannot change. But that they build nests in your hair, this you can prevent."

-Chinese proverb

Chapter 1

First Things First:
The Mirror Test

"A goal without a plan is just a wish."

-French writer and
aviator Antoine de Saint Exupery

Making changes in your life is not always easy. You have to decide that the change will be worth the effort—that the juice will be worth the squeeze.

As the first black player in Major League Baseball, Jackie Robinson withstood sickening harassment. "He had to be bigger than the Brooklyn teammates who got up a petition to keep him off the ball club," Hank Aaron recalled, "bigger than the pitchers who threw at him, bigger than the base runners who dug their spikes into his shins, and bigger than the so-called fans who mocked him with mops on their heads and wrote him death threats."

Robinson knew that his struggle was empowering the entire African-American community. Through it all, he rose above his enemies and kept his sense of humor. On the morning of his first appearance with the Dodgers, he kissed his wife goodbye at their hotel. "If you come to the field today you won't have any trouble recognizing me," he playfully remarked. "I'm number 42."

I did not choose this path in life. It chose me. I agonized about what had happened to my life. I could only choose to give up or keep fighting. I decided that I wanted a rematch in the game of life, and this time I was going to win. I knew that I was going to come out on top because I was willing to do whatever was necessary.

The mirror test

How can you know where you want to go if you don't know where—or who—you are? Before you do anything else, I recommend that you take an inventory of your life. Gaining clarity is critical to your success, and the following inventories will show you where you are on your road to happiness.

The mirror test is an exercise that helps you discover your strengths and weaknesses. I call it the mirror test because you have to look yourself in the mirror and make an honest appraisal of your life. Some of the things that you find may shock you. You will probably find issues that you were afraid to discover. It is all part of the process. You have to find the problems in your life so that you can deal with them head on.

Rate the following areas of your life from 1-10 (1 being the lowest, 10 being the highest), then add up your scores to see where you stand:

1.	Work	(__/10)
2.	Family	(__/10)
3.	Social Life	(__/10)
4.	Finances	(__/10)
5.	Health/Fitness	(__/10)
6.	Spirituality	(__/10)
7.	Emotions	(__/10)
8.	Education	(__/10)
9.	Work-Life Balance	(__/10)
10.	Stress Management/Humor	(__/10)

Total (__/100)

10-49:   "Trouble is brewing…"

Your life feels like a terminal illness. You are working on a nervous breakdown—if you are not already there. You feel like you don't measure up and you cannot catch a break. Every situation is another prayer unanswered. You are surviving, but you are not living. You have a long way to go to find happiness, but do not get discouraged. Focus on taking small steps in the right direction.

50-69:   "Stuck in a rut…"

There are more question marks in your life than exclamation points. Some areas of your life make you happy, while other areas are nuisances that drain you of your passion and your energy. Problem areas in your life feel like huge hurdles that you have to get over. You are living a less-than-life. The weak areas of your life are in need of a serious overhaul. Use the information in this book as the foundation for a new and improved you.

70-89:   "It could be worse…"

The majority of your hopes and aspirations have gone from "I think I can" to "I knew I could." At the same time, you view failures and accidents as opportunities for growth. You have a very fulfilling life, but there is a nagging feeling that it could be better. The key is to make sure that you do not settle into a complacent life. Your life is already good. Why not make it great.

90-100: "On cloud nine…"

You are one of the lucky few. You have found the location of true happiness—between your ears. You wake up every morning with a smile on your face and a story to tell. When you look back on your life, you realize that you have been truly blessed. Feel free to close this book and move on. There is very little that I could say that will help you, because you do not need much help—if any help at all. Perhaps I should be coming to you for advice instead of the other way around.

This exercise is designed to show you that the key to true health and happiness is balance. Think of your life as a chain, and each of these ten points as links in that chain. No matter how strong the other nine links are, the chain will only be as strong as the weakest link. It doesn't matter if you have a great job if you are missing the support of family and friends. All the money in the world is worthless if you have to lose your physical health to get it. It is also hard to enjoy a good social life at night if you spend every day at a job that you despise.

To give you an idea of the kind of changes that are possible with the information contained in these pages, my mirror test score went from a 48 before writing this book to an 88 after following this program to the letter. I am not going to pretend that my life is perfect. I live three hours away from my parents, I wish that I had a degree in religious studies, and I would love to have children. My life hasn't reached its fairy tale ending, but it is a lot closer. I expect the same type of results for you as well.

Reader, know thyself

The next step is to take an inventory of who you are and what you want to become. These are questions that you must answer for yourself. Take this as an opportunity to get to know the real you a little better:

- What makes you happy?

_____

_____

_____

_____

- What makes you unhappy?

_____

_____

_____

- What do you need to do to become the kind of person that you want to be?

_____

_____

_____

- What would you be doing differently if you did not have to worry about anything?

_____

_____

_____

- In what ways do you take your life too seriously?

_____

_____

_____

- In what ways do you take yourself too seriously?

_____

_____

_____

- What should you thank God for today?

_____

_____

_____

- What are the last two selfless acts that you have performed?

_____

_____

_____

- How do others describe you?

_____

_____

_____

Goal setting

Each of us has a vision of how wonderful our life could be. Oftentimes the hard part is not reaching that vision, but deciding exactly what that vision is. Get in a life-changing mood by painting a picture in your mind of the life that your heart desires. Do some research and planning to determine what you optimistically—yet realistically—want to have, to attain, to possess, and to be. Recording your goals and priorities is a great way to ensure that you do not do anything for lack of a better idea. You can use these goals as the roadmap to a life of passion and happiness.

> "You can't build a reputation on what you're going to do."
>
> -Automaker Henry Ford

What are your top five goals for the next six months?

1. _____

    _____

    _____

2. _____

    _____

    _____

3. _____
   _____
   _____

4. _____
   _____
   _____

5. _____
   _____
   _____

What are your top five goals for the next year?

1. _____
   _____
   _____

2. _____
   _____
   _____

3. _____
   _____
   _____

4. _____
   _____
   _____

5. _____
   _____
   _____

What are your top five goals for the next five years?

1. _____

   _____

   _____

2. _____

   _____

   _____

3. _____

   _____

   _____

4. _____

   _____

   _____

5. _____

   _____

   _____

What are your top five goals for the next twenty years?

1. _____

   _____

   _____

2. _____

   _____

   _____

3. _____

   _____

   _____

4. _____

   _____

   _____

5. _____

   _____

   _____

Do something with this info

You are reading this book because there are things in your life that have not gone as planned. Now is the time to make your comeback. As my football coach would always remind us: "It's gut check time." You have already made some progress. Now you know where you are and where you want to be. But, talk is cheap and well-done is always better than well-said. It is the actions that you take from this moment on that matter the most.

When something energizes you, pursue it. When something drains you, step back. You may experience some uncomfortable growing pains. Nevertheless, ask yourself if you want these changes bad enough. Even the hard times can be approached with a good attitude when they are part of your master plan.

"Either we will find a way or we will make one."

-Hannibal, speaking of crossing the Alps

Create a support system

You cannot do this alone. This I know. That is why I surround myself with people who care about me and are not afraid to help me deal with the issues that I am confronted with. You have been there for other people in the past. Now it is time for other people to be there for you.

Support groups are popular because they work. They allow you to bring your problems out into the open and focus on solutions. The moment that you tell your goals to the world, they become real and attainable. There is no more someday. It is much easier to stick to a plan if you have someone holding your feet to the fire. A strong support system will ensure your success.

Questions that you should ask when choosing someone to hold you accountable:

1. Do they care about you and want what is best for you?
2. Are they willing to read—or at least skim through—this book so that they know what you are trying to accomplish?
3. Are they willing to call or visit you on a regular basis to monitor your progress?
4. Are they willing to be honest and stern with you when they feel that you are slacking?
5. Do they know you well enough to understand which parts of your life are in need of a change?

Life Lessons:

- The mirror test is an exercise to help you discover your strengths and weaknesses by appraising your life. The first step towards "fixing" your life is to figure out what is broken.
- Many people are shocked to find out how little they know about themselves. Find out who you are so that you can decide who you hope to become. Set real and attainable goals that will make you the best person that you can be.
- Accountability and support are the keys to your success or failure. Your loved ones can motivate you and keep you progressing towards your goals. Tough times don't seem so tough when you have the right people in your corner.

Chapter 2

Relax or Perish: Seven Steps to Stress Management

> "When I look back on all the worries, I remember the story of the old man who said on his deathbed that he had had a lot of trouble in his life, most of which never happened."
>
> -Winston Churchill

Imagine a time thousands of years ago. You are a caveman stalking ten thousand pounds of woolly mammoth. You are poised to attack, but it is a risky proposition. Either you or the beast will go home well fed today. Your heartbeat is steadily increasing. Your muscles become tight and tense. You are more aware of the sun on the horizon and the spear in your hand. You make your move, and it is finished. Your prey lies at your feet, and you relax as you prepare your celebratory feast.

This primitive survival mechanism—the "fight-or-flight" stress response—is programmed into every human being. It responds to everything from escaping a burning building to having your marketing proposal ready for next week's staff meeting.

Decades of brain research has revealed that humans are hard-wired for stress through an intricate pattern of neural pathways designed to deal with stressful situations and quickly return to normal. Although this stress response is helpful and necessary when dealing with short-lived stressors, issues result when the stress— or the perceived stress—remains for long periods. It is similar to a racecar driver who constantly pushes his car too hard. A blown engine is the inevitable conclusion.

Fast forward to present-day, and stress is a huge issue in America. It is everywhere. It burdens us at work. It hurts our relationships. Ironically, it even shares a bed with us. The stress may be less life threatening than stalking a prehistoric beast, but it is just as real. What makes stress so deadly today is that we wake up with it the day after we graduate from college, and it stays with us until the day we retire—or die—whichever comes first.

"Stress is when you wake up screaming, and then realize that you haven't fallen asleep yet."

-Author Unknown

Unless the body has a chance to recover, the effects of stress tend to accumulate and build up. This can lead to a variety of symptoms, such as:

Irritability

Frequent Colds/Flu

Fatigue

Depression

Stomach problems

Impaired memory

Weight Gain

High Blood Pressure

Restless sleep

Chronic pain

Asthma

Allergies

Insomnia

High Cholesterol

Reduced Sex Drive

Chronic stress is a killer that can wreak havoc on your health. America spent 2.3 trillion dollars on health care in 2007—more than we spent on food.[1] Stress is a major contributing factor to that bill. There is cause for concern, but stress doesn't have to be a death sentence. How you manage your stress has the potential to add years to your life, and life to your years.

De-stress and decompress

Webster's dictionary defines stress as a mentally or emotionally disruptive influence. The rest of the world defines it as working fifty hours a week, taking care of two kids, and fighting with your spouse about the bills. Or, as the author Natalie Goldberg put it: "Stress is an ignorant state. It believes that everything is an emergency."

The truth about stress is that it is only an influence. Stress is not a thing; it is a reaction. The difference between the amount of stress you perceive and the actual stress itself depends on your state of mind. Something that feels highly stressful to one person—public speaking or bull fighting—is exhilarating to another.

When we take this fresh look at stress, we begin to see where it really comes from—our own thoughts. Once you redefine stress as something that you can control it changes everything. You can analyze any situation and ease off the pressure wherever possible. The following program will help.

Dr. O's seven-step stress reduction program

Stress related symptoms are very common, but that does not make them normal. There will inevitably be times in your life when you go through high-stress situations. It may be several times a year; it may be several times a minute. Nevertheless, there is hope.

Stress does not have to consume your life. There are seven strategies that can minimize the physical, mental, and emotional damage that comes with your day-to-day stress.

1. Journaling

This is a simple way to deal with stress. If you are anything like me, you have trouble falling asleep when something is weighing on your mind. Try this simple technique. Put your thoughts down on paper before bed. This will take the worry out of your mind, and put it on the page. Let the journal worry about it for the night.

I also like to talk into a tape recorder whenever I have something on my mind. This is especially true while I am driving. It allows me to process my thoughts and get on with my day. It is somehow calming to know that my problems will be waiting for me when I am in a better frame of mind to deal with them.

> Action steps: Get a journal and a digital audio recorder. Use them whenever you need to get a burden off your chest.

2. Laughter

Whoever said that laughter is the best medicine was quite wise. People with a strong sense of humor live longer and suffer from less chronic diseases than their less jovial friends. Laughter is God's hand on a trouble world. When you are laughing, there is no other emotion in that moment except joy. No anger, no depression, no fear—only joy. Use this to your advantage and laugh as much as you can.

Everyone has their own unique sense of humor. I can't tell you what you think is funny. This is something that you will have to decide for yourself. However, I have some ideas: go to a comedy club, make up funny stories with your loved ones, watch a funny movie, have a tickle fight, or keep a book of jokes in your desk at work.

Action steps: Do something that makes you laugh whenever you can. For starters, watch anything with Chris Farley or Bill Murray in it. Might I recommend *Caddyshack.*

3. Get a fun hobby

When I first started my private practice, I was as stressed as I had ever been. I had to make a decision. I had to find something to help me deal with my stress, or I had to look for a different career. I needed to find a hobby.

After several unsuccessful attempts—including learning how to play the guitar and playing the card game euchre on the internet—I found the perfect cure for what ailed me; cycling. After a long day at the office, I would put on my headphones, find a trail, and pedal my worries away.

When you try to find the best hobby for you, keep this in mind. Pick something that you truly enjoy. I quit playing the guitar when I felt like I was pressuring myself to do it. Whatever you choose must bring you pure enjoyment. Many people enjoy writing, knitting, playing board games, or reading. Whatever you enjoy, give yourself some time to relax, unwind, and decompress. While it may take some getting used to, it will be worth it.

Action Steps: Find something that you love. Make time for it whenever you can. The dishes will wait, your happiness will not. Concentrate on the enjoyment of the activity, not the fact that it might be taking you away from something that you "should" be doing.

4. Exercise

When you feel good, good things happen. Multiple studies have shown that exercise can be as effective as prescription antidepressants for treating anxiety and depression.[2] Exercise burns off the stress hormones that build up in your body. It also floods your body with the mood-enhancing endorphins that are responsible for the "runner's high" that causes a sense of calm to wash over you. Another positive stress-reducing benefit of exercise is that it improves your self-image and makes you feel better about yourself.

When exercising to help combat stress, the key is to pick something that is enjoyable. If you start an exercise program that you don't enjoy, it will be counterproductive and lead to more stress. Try something fun like tennis, swimming, or salsa dancing.

It is also important to exercise at the right time of day. If possible, exercise right after work. It acts as a bridge between your work life and your home life. Leave the stress of the day on the treadmill so that you do not take it out on your loved ones.

Action Steps: See your doctor to make sure that you are healthy enough to begin an exercise regimen. Start by taking a walk with someone you love. Get a gym membership. Try something new. Most importantly, break a sweat with a smile on your face.

---

5. Quiet Time

As simple as this sounds, most people forget to put their brains in neutral every once in a while. In this age of technology and convenience, you would think that we would have hours of free time every day. It has not really panned out that way. We are lucky to find time for sleep after ten hours of work, shuttling the kids to their activities, preparing dinner, paying the bills, and picking up the dry cleaning. Quiet time is usually put off until tomorrow. Even when we "relax", we do not give our brains a rest. We are either worrying about the future or we are mesmerized by the television.

Your brain is just like any other part of your body. It will wear out if it does not get a break. You have to tap on the brakes several times a day. There are many ways to accomplish this. Some pray while others meditate. Some people stare out the window. The great thing is that it does not matter what you do (or don't do). This is especially important for people who work outside of the home. Spend a few minutes unwinding so that your work stress doesn't follow you through the front door.

Action Steps: Take a brain-free break every day. Hang a beautiful picture in your office and stare at it. Take the scenic route home from work. Close your eyes in your driveway for five minutes before you enter your home. Remind yourself that sometimes you need to relax and "try easier."

6. Talk to someone

This is another way to get your problems out of your mind and off of your back. Call a friend or family member, find a support group, go to a therapist, or talk to God. You cannot survive if you let the stress build up. Women live longer than men do because as a rule they express their feelings more freely. They do not carry the weight of the world on their shoulders. Talking to someone is a great way to vent out the pressure.

My life has been extremely blessed in many ways. Without question, I have been blessed in this area more than any other. My family and friends have given me all of the support that I have ever needed. Some have been the voice of reason. Others have shown me unconditional love. Still others have been my rock, a sturdy surface to lean on in my darkest hours. I have had many high points in my life, and I credit the broad shoulders of my loved ones for all of my success.

Action Steps: Establish a support network of people that you trust. Use them as an ear to bend, but remember to return the favor when necessary.

7. Prayer

I enjoy talking to God about my problems. His answers are always very helpful if you know how to listen. Prayer can be seen as a spiritual form of meditation, and it leaves you feeling powerful—yet humbled. God speaks to you through the Holy Bible. He expects you to return the favor by spending time in His presence.

> Action Steps: Make the time to thank your God for all that He has given you. Remember that you always have someone to talk to.

From lemons to lemonade

I wish that this book did not exist. If my life went as planned, I never would have begun the transformation that turned into *Never Enough*. This book came forth from the ashes of a shattered life. If I had not become physically ill and mentally exhausted, you would not know that I exist. Every personal tragedy, every failed relationship, every bad career decision, and every health problem has led me to this moment. I now know that my life was assisting me when it seemed to be working against me. The troubling events that I experienced in the valleys of my life have led me to a mountain of happiness and peace.

Deciding to be happy is the first step to becoming happy. You will be much better off if you are willing to turn the lemons that life gives you into lemonade. Almost any bad thing that happens in your life has the potential to be a blessing in disguise. There are examples of this all around us. You just have to keep your heart and mind open to change.

> "The time to relax is when you don't have time for it."
>
> -American journalist Sydney J. Harris

Life Lessons:

- The fight-or-flight stress response is designed to deal with stressful situations and quickly return to normal. What makes stress a killer is that we have to deal with too much of it without any practical strategies to eliminate it.
- Chronic stress contributes to most of today's health problems. Our body is built for a stress sprint, but we live in a stress marathon. Unless we have a chance to recover, the effects of stress will build up until it is too late. You can only bend so much before you break.
- Stress does not have to consume your life. Stress reduction programs can minimize the physical, mental, and emotional damage that stress can cause. While you cannot avoid stressful situations, you can learn how to deal with them in a healthier manner.
- One of the most important strategies to live a less stressful life is to learn how to look at life with an optimistic point of view. Try to find the positive in every obstacle that you are faced with. When you face a difficult situation, tell yourself: "Something is going to kill me, but it will not be this, and it will not be today."

Chapter 3

Pull the Plug: Television's Influence on Your Life

"All television is educational television. The question is: what is it teaching?"

-Former FCC commissioner Nicholas Johnson

What would you pay for a three-step program that will add twelve years to your life? Would you mortgage your home? Would you sell your car? Would you sell your most prized possessions? Well, don't sell your fine china or your baseball cards just yet. Consider this my gift to you:

The Life Extension Program:

Step 1: Stand up
Step 2: Walk towards your television
Step 3: Pull plug vigorously

I am making light of the situation, but the problems with television are no laughing matter. The average American watches more than four hours of television each day.[3] That is twenty-eight hours a week, two months a year, or twelve years of nonstop television watching over a seventy-two year lifespan. While you may enjoy your TV time, I am guessing that you would give anything to put that sand back in the hourglass as you near the end of your life. Imagine how much fuller and more productive your life could be if you used that time wisely. You could go back to school, perform at the community theatre, or be a better spouse and parent.

There are so many things in life that we put off because we do not think that we have enough time. I am sure that you have said something like, "I'll start as soon as things settle down at work," or, "I'm too busy now but maybe after I retire." Blaming your lack of productivity on a lack of time is a flimsy excuse as long as you are spending your leisure time sitting on the couch.

Another problem with television is that while its manufactured experiences make you feel comfortable and safe, it tends to separate you from the outside world. Television viewers become spectators, with no chance for self-expression or self-discovery. Television and movies portray such a narrow spectrum of human experience that we have forgotten how smart, strong, creative, and loving human beings can be. I have given up on the "idiot box" because I crave these types of real experiences.

> "Television has changed a child from an irresistible force to an immovable object."
>
> -Author unknown

Television's effect on our culture

The question is not whether television viewing comes with a price. The question is how much. If only two hundred million Americans watch four hours of TV per day, it would add up to nearly three hundred billion hours of television per year. Instead of engaging in productive activities that improve our lives, we are sitting on our sofa (from Italy) watching a DVD (from Taiwan) on our television (from Japan). Is there any wonder that our marriages are ending, our children are obese, and our jobs are heading oversees?

When you watch television, you are the target of images of more—and better—products than what you own. You will be exposed to millions of commercials in your lifetime, and advertisers work very hard to keep you from being satisfied. You are bombarded with images of people richer and happier than you are. New and improved products herald the promise of a better life. This increases the desire for material possessions and reminds you that your life is not good enough. You will always need more money so that you can buy more stuff.

Television does more than influence your time and your money. Television influences your thinking. It changes your aspirations and the value that you place on morality. It changes how you feel about superficial beauty. It changes how you feel about your fellow man. Television glorifies danger over compassion, sex over love, and violence over respect. It is crucial that you back away from the TV to keep it from skewing your thinking.

Television is bad because it makes you hate your house and your washing machine. It is worse because it tries to make you hate yourself. Television has changed the way that people feel about themselves. It has altered our sense of self-esteem and self-worth.

There was a time when people were judged by their heart and the content of their character (thank you Dr. King). Now society judges people by their bra size and their body fat percentage. According to information compiled by TV Free America, female actors are 23% thinner than the average woman is, and they are thinner than 95% of the female population as a whole.[4] Meanwhile weight loss has become a 42 billion dollar industry[5] and eating disorders like anorexia and bulimia are more prevalent than ever. Many young women are having plastic surgery to look like Angelina Jolie, while their brothers are taking anabolic steroids to try to look like their favorite professional wrestler. Television has created an image that is nearly impossible to attain. Many people die trying.

Many young children are becoming a victim of the zombification of America as well. According to the A.C. Nielsen Company, children spend nine hundred hours per year using their brains in school, while they spend over fifteen hundred hours per year numbing them in front of the TV. They also found that parents spend less than four minutes per week in meaningful conversation with their children.[6] So who is really raising your kids? Is it you, or is it Homer Simpson and Hannah Montana?

> "Television has proved that people will look at anything rather than each other."
>
> -Advice columnist Ann Landers

Exceptions to the rule

Television is not inherently evil. It has the potential to inspire us and teach us valuable life lessons. Some programs deliver messages that can have a positive impact. My neighbor feels that the time she invests in Oprah and Martha Stewart Living is time well spent. I for one had given up on news media until I saw the refreshingly honest views of Jon Stewart and Stephen Colbert. Others use the advice of television personalities like Joyce Meyer and Suze Orman to improve their spiritual and financial futures. However, I do not see how the majority of television—celebrity gossip shows, soap operas, professional wrestling, and shows where people eat rotten pig guts for money—can make us happier people in a better world.

The unprecedented success of reality television is concrete proof of this. The majority of reality TV programming is little more than participants degrading themselves in front of a strategically placed camera crew—bringing the world along for the ride. Viewers watch other people live their lives instead of experiencing their own. They watch people travel to exotic locations instead of planning a weekend getaway. They watch chefs prepare five course meals while eating a frozen pizza. This is no way to live. We need to quit escaping into the lives of strangers and start to live our own.

"I can quit watching any time I want."

We know that watching television is not a productive way to spend our time. Yet we continue to do so much of it. The reality is that cutting back on TV watching may be as difficult as trying to give up cigarettes or rocky road ice cream.

According to Robert Kubey—a psychologist at Rutgers University—millions of Americans are so hooked on television that they actually fit the criteria for substance abuse. Heavy television viewers exhibit as many as six dependency symptoms—two more than necessary to arrive at a clinical diagnosis of substance abuse.[7] See if any of these remind you of yourself or someone that you love:

1. Using TV as a sedative:

- Do you watch TV when you need to relax?
- Do you fall into a trance while spending another weekend afternoon on the couch?
- Do you watch TV if you are having trouble sleeping?

2. Indiscriminate viewing:

- Do you watch reruns of television programs you have already seen multiple times?
- Have you ever developed "channel changers" thumb from overuse of the remote control?
- Have you ever caught yourself being sucked into an infomercial for a product that you would never buy?

3. Feeling angry with oneself for watching too much:

- Are you upset on Monday morning when you look back at how much of your weekend you spent watching television?
- Do you regret leaving your to-do list undone while you watch Seinfeld reruns?

4. Inability to stop watching:

- Do you have the TV on from the moment you wake up until the moment you fall asleep?

- Do you watch TV even though it is hurting your relationships with your family and friends?

5. Feeling miserable when kept from watching:

- Do you feel lost when the cable is out or your TV is broken?
- Would you have a nervous breakdown if you found out that your vacation resort does not have cable?

6. Feeling a loss of control while viewing:

- Do you feel an excessively strong emotional connection to the characters on your favorite TV programs?
- Do you care less about what is on, and more about what else is on?

If you answered yes to more than half of these questions, you may have a serious problem with the role that television plays in your life.

Cut the cord

You do not have to move to Amish country and give up television altogether. A television-free life is not for everyone, including myself. I get a lot of enjoyment out of watching sports and funny movies. However, I know that I have to be careful not to watch too much. The best thing for me is to watch television in moderation. It is a treat for me, not a staple of my life. I am no longer addicted to it like a drug. It has lost its grasp on my leisure time. If you follow the action steps that I have outlined, TV will lose its hold on you as well.

Dr. O's prescription for a TV-free life

1. Start with a viewing inventory

Make a list of the television programs that you watch for seven days. At the end of the week, label each program as productive or non-productive. Try not to look at your list with rose-colored glasses. Be honest with yourself. If you watch a documentary about global warming, I would call it productive. If you watch an infomercial about a new juicer, I would not.

2. Wean yourself off of the non-productive programs you are watching

There is nothing wrong with a movie night with the family. Use it as family bonding time. Just try not to get sucked into the programs that ask you to tune in at a set time every day or every week.

Go through your viewing inventory. Pick one day of the week where you will not watch the programs you rated as nonproductive. Once you start to build momentum, pick a second day, and so on. I have progressed to the point that I do not watch television from Monday through Thursday. It is not always easy, but it is worth it. Feel free to keep your favorite program or two. There is no need to eliminate everything. Moderation is the key.

> "I have never seen a bad television program, because I refuse to. God gave me a mind and a wrist that turns things off."
>
> -Talk show host Jack Paar

3. Have a TV intervention for the entire family

It will be much easier to make positive changes if you make it a family affair. Explain to your loved ones that you value your relationships with them more than anything on television. Have the entire family complete a viewing inventory, and decide as a family which days you will unplug the television.

4. Find a more productive use of your time

Most people who quit smoking will chew gum or suck on peppermint sticks to replace their cigarettes. Most people that are on a diet will munch on carrot sticks or rice cakes to keep out of the candy dish. Television can be just as addictive. It will help to replace your TV watching time with something that will add more value to your life. Here are a few examples:

- Put your library card to good use
- Spend an evening volunteering at the soup kitchen
- Take a walk
- Join a book club
- Try the lost art of letter writing
- Take your spouse dancing
- Get a karaoke machine
- Ponder your existence

> "I find television very educating. Every time somebody turns on the set, I go into the other room and read a book."
>
> -Comedian Groucho Marx

5. Turn the TV off when you are engaged in other tasks

Writing is one of the most relaxing and enjoyable things that I can do with my time. When I first started writing, I was surprised at how slow I was progressing, and how uninspiring the words were on the page. Then it hit me. I was writing about relaxation and simplifying life—and I was not doing either of them. I was trying to get my creative juices flowing, but I was allowing the TV to steal my focus. I was letting Bob Barker and the Chicago Cubs keep me from one of my dreams. I started writing in a more relaxing location and my writing was transformed immediately.

Multitasking has no place in your leisure time. There is nothing relaxing about trying to read or have a conversation with the television on in the background. TV is an interruption that keeps you from focusing on what you are trying to enjoy. Your mind is already running a thousand miles an hour; give it a break. Do not be afraid to be alone with your thoughts. Give the book or puzzle that you are working on the attention it deserves. You will be surprised at how much more relaxing and productive your time will be.

6. Get rid of your TV for a set amount of time

A few years ago, I met a man in a Christian men's group that shared that he and his wife got rid of their television for the first year of their marriage. They felt that it would help them grow deeper in love with one another. It worked. They have now been married for over twenty years, and they have never owned a TV.

I had to try it for myself. I decided on a six-month hiatus. I needed to break the hold that my television had on me. I had nothing to lose. It was extremely difficult to pack up my television, my DVD collection, and my video games. I spent a lot of time staring at the ceiling and re-reading old magazines for the first couple of weeks. I seriously doubted that I was going to make it. Thankfully, I stuck it out.

By the end of the sixth month, I felt like a new man. I was reading two books a week. I began writing in my journal again. I was preparing meals that required more than a microwave. I was taking a walk around a beautiful lake twice a week. I was happy. Going without television had started as a test of my will. It ended up awakening me to many of the principles that are in this book.

Maybe six months without television is too big of a commitment. Try a month or two. The television has taken enough time away from your life. Take a little of it back.

7. Find someone who will help keep you accountable

Accountability is one of your strongest allies. It is much harder to break a promise to a friend than it is to break a promise to yourself. Have a friend that has read this chapter stop by for surprise television inspections. Make a game of it, complete with an incentive or prize. If your friend catches you watching television, you owe them a home cooked meal, or something of the sort. Be creative, and have fun with it. That is what life is all about anyhow.

Life Lessons:

- The twelve years of television that the average person watches in their lifetime is a huge burden on our society and culture. It wastes so much of our time that we are buried beneath the sand in our hourglass.
- Advertisers make a very nice living making you feel uncomfortable about your body, your financial situation, and your possessions. Every time you watch TV, you give them a little more control over your life.
- Television is a lot harder to give up than you think. It takes a solid plan and a strong dose of willpower. However, if you are willing to make the sacrifice, you will be happier and better off for it.
- It is better to make the TV-free life a family affair. Get everyone involved. They may drag their feet for a while, but they will thank you someday.

Chapter 4

Less Is More: Time Management Techniques

> "I have learned to seek my happiness by limiting my desires, rather than in attempting to satisfy them."
>
> -British economist John Stuart Mill

We live in a world of excess. We work too much. We think too much. We do too much. We live life like hamsters on a wheel—running feverishly, in a hurry to get nowhere. Not only are we too busy to stop and smell the roses, we don't even know that they exist. The war for your time is never won, and your mind and body pay the ultimate price.

Everyone desires more flexibility and freedom. Now is the time to make it happen. Simplify your life and drop the dead weight that is holding you back. You can buy more time by clearing your cluttered schedule, cleaning up your cluttered finances, and most importantly, calming your cluttered mind.

Your cluttered mind

You create your experiences through your thinking. Your feelings and perceptions are all relative to your circumstances. Compare the difference between a leisurely twelve-mile ride home from work and a twelve-mile race to the next rest stop when your bladder is ready to burst. One is quick; the other seemingly takes an eternity. The only difference is between your ears. By changing the way that you see things, you can change how you feel about them.

What your brain processes becomes your emotions, perceptions, behaviors, and decisions. Often times our minds are running to a negative place—a past regret or a future worry. Cut the negative thoughts out of your mind and save your mental energy for positive thinking. Quit trying to make sure that nothing goes wrong, and appreciate the many things that are going right.

Another problem is that our thoughts are constantly running a mile a minute. The human brain is the most complicated system on the planet, yet we find a way to turn it into mush by trying to run it in high gear every waking moment. Learning how to calm your mind down and focus on one thing at a time is the key to tapping into your brains extraordinary abilities.

Take the brain of a professional baseball player for example. What is remarkable about them is not in their muscles or their joints; it is in their brain. They have the ability to make their brains work quicker than yours and mine.

Consider what Dr. Robert Adair, the Sterling Professor of Physics at Yale, says about hitting a baseball. He has shown that a fastball thrown at 95 mph will reach home plate—60 feet, 6 inches away— in less than four-tenths of a second. When a big-league pitch is on its way, the hitter has only about two-tenths of a second from the time the ball leaves the pitchers hand to process the last information that does them any conceivable good whatsoever,[8] and then swing a round bat at precisely the right time to hit a round ball in precisely the right place.

"If a person from another planet was told what's involved ... they would say it's impossible," says Porter Johnson, a physics professor at the Illinois Institute of Technology in Chicago. At least now I don't feel as bad about my feeble career in Little League baseball.

If it should be physically impossible to hit a baseball, how do professional hitters do it so well? They know how to let their brains take over by taking their foot off the gas. They block out all of their thoughts and fears, and let their brains make the calculations and decisions that are necessary. They turn the act of hitting a baseball into a reflex instead of a choice. That is why they say that a full mind is an empty bat. The lesson; if your overactive mind is wandering, you are doomed from the start.

The paradox of over-thinking is that you do not allow your brain to function at its best. Jonis Agee, author and literature professor at the University of Nebraska, says it best. She believes that we get our best ideas in the three B's: the bed, the bathtub, and the bus. It is unbelievable how well our brains operate in these types of situations. The common thread in these environments is that our unconscious mind takes over. Your brain is much smarter than you are. The key is to get out of its way and allow it to function at full throttle.

This has been proven time and time again in my own life. I get most of my "million dollar" ideas in the car because I have learned to take advantage of this type of thinking. I always have a digital tape recorder close by, especially for long trips. I used to record my thoughts in a journal while I drove, but it was starting to get dangerous. A digital recorder will allow you to keep track of your thoughts and ideas without wrapping your car around a tree.

Another way to clear your cluttered mind is to listen to your gut. Pay attention to that feeling that you get in the pit of your stomach. It is your soul screaming at you to do the right thing. I have made more mistakes than I would care to admit because I did not follow this advice. I spent too much time listening to my logical brain. My brain put me in the wrong city, the wrong profession, and the wrong relationship. Never allow logic to interfere with your heart and your soul. Learn to harness the power of your gut.

"Remember, happiness doesn't depend upon who you are or what you have, it depends solely upon what you think."

-Dale Carnegie

Your cluttered schedule

In 1976, the Staffordshire city council began receiving complaints that the cities buses often failed to stop for passengers, regularly sailing past lines of as many as thirty people. Councilor Arthur Chorlton addressed the complaints by explaining—with a straight face—that making such stops would disrupt the system's schedule.

How many times has your schedule seemed as unstoppable as these buses? We try to cram thirty hours worth of schedule into a twenty-four hour day. Our hectic pace saps our energy and undermines the quality of our lives. We fill our schedules to the brim, neglecting to factor in that we are often at the mercy of other people. How will your tight schedule be affected if you are stuck in traffic, your dentist is running thirty minutes late, or your boss asks you to work on Saturday? Wouldn't it be nice to create a little breathing room? If you use the following three-step plan to take control of your schedule, traffic jams and scheduling conflicts will not ruin your day and spoil your mood.

"Calendars are for careful people, not passionate ones."

-American poet Carl Sandburg

Step 1: The Time-use log

The reason that you are not where you want to be is that you are not doing the things that you want to do. Your schedule is full of nonproductive and nonessential activities that steal the most precious resource that you have—your time.

You cannot save time until you know how you are spending it. Begin by recording your daily activities so that you can step outside of yourself to see what your life really looks like. Keep an hourly log of every activity you perform for seven to fourteen days, whichever gives you the best representation of your regular schedule.

Once the time-use log is completed, you can see where your time is going. Break your time up into as many categories as you feel are necessary to paint an accurate picture. Be as specific as you wish, but be sure to note how much time you spend in the following major areas:

- Work
- Sleep
- TV watching
- Driving
- Family time
- Fun
- Time for yourself

Add up the number of hours that you spend in each category. If you are performing more than one activity at a time, divide the time up as best as you can. For example, if you are watching television for an hour while paying the bills, you could split the time into thirty minutes for each activity. Just be as honest with yourself as you can.

After you have finished dissecting your schedule, you should be able to determine whether or not your life is balanced between work, sleep, and play. Some people are going to find worse problems here than others. The first time I did this exercise, I nearly fainted. My 168-hour week went as follows:

Work:	80 hours
Sleep:	42 hours
TV watching:	21 hours
Driving:	3.5 hours
Family time:	6 hours
Fun:	12 hours
Time for myself:	3.5 hours

Some observations that I made:
- My work was taking up nearly half of my life, and it was taking up two-thirds of my waking hours

- I was spending as much time in my car as I was spending on quality time for myself
- I was losing two days worth of sleep every week

Compare my old schedule to the most recent time I performed this exercise:

Work (including writing):   29.5 hours
Sleep: 56 hours
TV watching: 7 hours
Driving: 10 hours
Family time: 26 hours
Fun: 29 hours
Time for myself: 10.5 hours

I am sure that you can guess by comparing my two schedules that I am much happier and healthier now than I was the first time I completed this exercise. I finally have enough time to do the things that make me happy. I get to recharge my batteries at night, and I feel like I am squeezing ever minute out of my days.

Common problems and solutions

This is a very individual experience. Your work situation, commute time, and social calendar are different from mine. However, several issues are common to the majority of us. The following five problems show up in the majority of the time-use logs that I see. The number in parenthesis indicates the percent of the time that I encounter them.[9]

1. Watching too much television (91%)

For the purpose of this study, too much television is more than sixty minutes a day. Every hour that you are watching television is an hour that you could be doing something more productive, like spending time with your family, exercising, enjoying a fun hobby, or sleeping.

I am amazed at how much easier it is for me to complete my to-do list when I take television out of the equation. My house is clean, my work is done, and I have done it with time to spare. I end up having so much free time that I make myself a snack, settle into my favorite chair, and...read a book!

Action Steps: Turn off the television and better yourself. Find a productive replacement to fill your leisure time. Refer to chapter 3 for more ideas.

---

2. Getting less than eight hours of sleep (79%)

When I began my research I was beginning to wonder if anyone was getting the seven to nine hours of sleep that our bodies so desperately need. It was also obvious to me that our sleep issues stem from other lifestyle factors. We lose sleep because we work too many hours and we watch too much TV. We intend to get more sleep, but Martha Stewart is going to be on Late Night with Conan O'Brien tonight. We tell ourselves that we can always get more sleep tomorrow.

Action Steps: Turn off the television and get to bed. Take the television out of your bedroom. Do not bring work home with you. Develop a ritual to help you unwind before bed.

---

3. Working too many hours (73%)

I define too many hours of work as fifty-five or more hours of work per week, both inside and outside of the home. This includes your job, yard work, home and car maintenance, housework, and any other activity that you consider work, whether you are compensated for it or not.

Action Steps: Be more productive with your time at work so that you can minimize the late nights and the weekend overtime. Handle your money wisely, so that you can work less. Delegate household chores if help is available.

4. Neglecting to make time for fun (64%)

What is your life worth if you do not find time to laugh and play? Life is too short to spend your days doing things that you do not enjoy. You should be having fun at least two hours a day.

Life is not as black and white as the time-use log is trying to make it. Many of our day-to-day activities are shades of gray. For example, I think that gardening is fun. You may see it as work or maybe even quiet time. In the end, this is for your benefit, so categorize your time as you see fit.

Action Steps: Live the life that makes you as happy as possible. Find the comedy in every situation. Find hobbies that make you happy. Quit taking life so seriously; you will never get out alive.

5. Spending too much time in the car (17%)

I consider ninety minutes a day—the national average—to be too much time behind the wheel.[10] I list this problem with the others because I know that this is a much larger concern than my research has found. I conducted most of my surveys in small to medium sized cities in the Midwest where traffic is usually not an issue. It takes thirteen minutes to get from one side of the town that I live in to the other. The only way that you are going to be stuck in traffic is if you are stuck behind a tractor. This is very different from the traffic congestion that you would find in large metropolitan areas.

Another difficulty is determining how much of your driving time is non-productive. I average nearly two hours per day in the car due to my commute. However, I do not consider it a non-productive use of my time for several reasons. While I have to drive an hour to work, I am driving to a fifteen hour a week job. My commute time is much less than the number of work hours it allows me to save. I am also reimbursed for my mileage, which means that I am being paid for my time.

Action Steps: Find a job that is closer to home. Find a home that is closer to work. Find a job with a schedule that will allow you to miss rush hour traffic. Find a way to do some or all of your work from home.

Step 2: The Time Productivity Index

Now you know where your time is going. The next step is to find out how much of your time is being wasted by activities that are not enhancing your life. Do this by evaluating every activity that is on your time-use log. Ask yourself these potential life-changing questions during this process: What makes you happy? What puts you in a bad mood? What activities are helping you attain a better future? What activities bring meaning to your life?

As you go through your time-use inventory, label each activity as either:

PE = Productive and Essential

These are the basis of what makes your life yours. They benefit your life by making it better. These activities include sleep, exercise, working at a job that you love, bathing, and family time.

These are the activities that you need to maximize to make your life as pleasurable and plentiful as possible.

PN = Productive and Nonessential

These are the things that you give your time and attention to because you want to, not because you have to. You make time for these things because they make you happy. They include hobbies, volunteer work, church, and quiet time.

These are the activities that you need to make a conscious effort to do more of. You need to add these activities to your life by subtracting nonproductive activities from your schedule.

NE = Nonproductive and Essential

These are the activities that are a necessary part of your life, but they do not directly enhance it. These include activities like yard work, a long commute, working at a job that you do not enjoy, and car maintenance.

These are the things that you are going to minimize by delegation, creative thinking, and making the necessary life changes.

NN = Nonproductive and Nonessential

These are the pure time wasters in your life. They are the activities that you know are nonproductive, yet you do them anyway. These include watching reality television, drinking in excess, and surfing the internet.

These are the activities that you are going to eliminate to the fullest extent possible. You are going to take your life back from these time-parasites.

Note: This is a very subjective project. If you think something is productive, it is. If you think something is essential, it is. I just hope that you think bathing is essential.

Add up the total number of hours in each category. Divide each of these totals by 168—the number of hours in a week—and you have your time productivity index. Here is an example. This is the time productivity index of Liz, one of my former students—a 23-year-old female with a part-time job and no children:

Productive/Essential   PE: 91 hours per week / 168 = 54.2%
Productive/Nonessential   PN: 8 hours per week / 168 = 4.8%

Nonproductive/Essential   NE: 14 hours per week / 168 = 8.3%
Nonproductive/Nonessential   NN: 55 hours per week / 168 = 32.7%

At the end of the week, she felt that 41% of her schedule was nonproductive and 37.5% of her schedule was nonessential. Both of these numbers were higher than she expected—or wanted. She was wasting many of the 8760 hours that God had blessed her with for the year. The good news is that we were able to change things with very little effort. We will come back to her example after we finish step 3.

Step 3: Take back your life

Time is a lot like matter and energy. It cannot be created or destroyed; it can only be rearranged. The key is to move your time to activities that will better serve you.

Evaluate your time-use log. Create a list of things that you would like to do more of, and a second list of things that you would like to minimize or eliminate. Next to each item, create action steps that will help you accomplish these goals. These steps could be as simple as giving up one hour of television a week, or as difficult as quitting your job to find one that makes you happy. What you do with this information is completely up to you. I can only create the questions in your mind. You need to answer them for yourself.

Back to our example. After Liz completed this step, we agreed that there were changes she could make immediately that would have a positive effect on her life. She decided to:

- Take three additional credit hours of school per week to help her complete her degree program sooner.
- Spend three more hours a week studying to make the dean's list.
- Devote three hours a week to volunteering at the animal shelter.
- Find seven more hours a week to work on her hobbies—poetry and digital photography.
- Enjoy ten more hours of quality time with her family and friends every week.

- Eliminate twenty-six hours of television viewing, shopping, and computer usage a week to make room in her schedule for her new activities.

Liz's new time productivity index:

Productive/Essential   PE: 107 hours per week / 168 = 63.7%
Productive/Nonessential   PN: 18 hours per week / 168 = 10.7%
Nonproductive/Essential   NE: 14 hours per week / 168 = 8.3%
Nonproductive/Nonessential   NN: 29 hours per week / 168 = 17.3%

Her new schedule decreased her nonproductive time by 26 hours a week, and her nonessential time by 16 hours a week. The beautiful thing is that everything that was added to her calendar will make her life better, and nothing she got rid of will hurt her life at all. These are massive changes for anyone, especially for a college student. Liz is now extremely happy. She has altered the course of her life. Now it is your turn.

Under-schedule

I have done too many things in my life for the sole purpose of creating a socially acceptable persona. I went to all of the business networking events. I schmoozed at all of the right parties. I sacrificed my time to work with every charity and committee that approached me. I was doing an excellent job at playing the part of big-shot community leader, but I could not keep up the pace.

What made my hectic life even worse was that I didn't enjoy many of the things that I was doing. I was sacrificing the things that I enjoyed for the things that I was "supposed" to do. I was doing too many things that are not a part of who I am. I was trying to cram a square peg into a round hole, and I needed to find a way to take control of my life.

If you do not prioritize, your life can become overwhelming. Things will pile up until you are consumed. Consider the damage done to your schedule every time that you say yes to a new task without eliminating something that takes up the same amount of time. No raindrop believes it is to blame for the flood, and nothing on your schedule thinks that it is responsible for the problems in your life.

The treatment for this disease to please is as simple as the word no. If you can master the power of a compassionate "no, thank you," you will set yourself free. Sometimes you have to say no to good things. You might have to step away from a committee or take on fewer projects at work. You will have to quit helping others if it is hurting you and your family. Never make your family feel like they come second. You have to set boundaries and limits in every part of your life.

Now I focus on activities that bring me peace and happiness. I do the things that I want, not what society expects of me. I made myself miserable for years by trying to be who I thought I was supposed to be, not who I truly am. I felt like a typecast character in a bad movie. It was completely liberating once I understood that I could only do so much.

Seven tips for under-scheduling

1. Create a hierarchy in your life. Mine is God, then family, then me, and lastly work. Whenever asked to take on a new task, refer to this list to make sure that it is a good fit for your life.
2. Plan your errands and daily tasks in advance to maximize efficiency.
3. The laundry can wait, life cannot. Delegate activities like yard work, home repairs, and cleaning whenever possible.
4. Try to kill two birds with one stone. Create an exercise program that is also fun. Turn odd jobs around the house into family time. Keep a good book in the car to read while stuck in gridlock.
5. If you are going to watch TV, tape the programs you like so that you can watch them later. You can save seven or eight minutes every time you watch a thirty-minute program by fast-forwarding past the commercials.

6. Always leave a cushion between appointments so that they will not have to be rescheduled if you are running a few minutes late.
7. Make sure that everything you do is worth your time. If you don't really enjoy your weekly golf game, quit. If your bridge game has become a weekly gossip session, find something better to do.

Life Lessons:

- Set your brain free by listening to your gut and your unconscious mind. Get out of your own way when you have a question that needs answered.
- Take control of your schedule so that you can accomplish everything that you want with leisure time to spare. Quit trying to cram so much into your day. There is always tomorrow.
- Don't waste your time on activities that are nonproductive and nonessential. Every minute that you waste is a minute that could be put to good use.
- Prioritize your life so that you can focus on your happiness. Remember that the most powerful word in the English language is NO. Doing less gives you the opportunity to "be" more.

Chapter 5

Happiness Cannot be Bought: Managing Your Finances

> "It is pretty hard to tell what does bring happiness; poverty and wealth have both failed."
>
> -American playwright Kin Hubbard

According to USAToday.com, there were over 2 million bankruptcy petitions filed in federal courts in 2005, up from 1.5 million bankruptcies in 2004. We save less than we should and spend more than we ought. Many people are one pink slip or hospital bill away from financial ruin. How are they supposed to keep their head above water when they are sinking in a sea of debt?

It is becoming increasingly difficult to be a member of the lower-middle to middle class. You don't make enough money to get ahead in life, but you make too much money to get assistance from government programs. The secret is to take one step back now so that you can take two steps forward in the future. While you may not live in as nice of a house, you will have a better home life. While you may not drive as nice of a car, you will not be driving your loved ones crazy by arguing about money. You will have money tucked away so that you are not in financial distress.

The first thing to do is to look at money in a new light. If you are consumed by the need for money and material things, this book will be of little value to you. There are numerous books on financial success and climbing over people on the corporate ladder. This is not one of them. This book is about becoming a success at the game of life, regardless of the number of zeroes on your paycheck. Don't get me wrong, I still play the lottery. Money is just further down on my list of priorities than it used to be. I have gotten the money part out of my system. I do not need a bigger house or a faster car. I am at a point where I focus on living, not owning.

One of the most powerful moments in my life was when I discovered what my accountant meant when he said that it is better to sleep well than to eat well. I learned that material goods would never bring me peace and contentment. The pursuit of money kept me from the pursuit of happiness. I gave too much of my time to my work, and I have lost important relationships because of it. I hurt my family in the present because I was working so hard to improve our future. King Solomon's gold could not make it worth the pain that I put my loved ones through. They have forgiven me; I just hope that I can forgive myself.

"Happiness depends, as nature shows, less on exterior things than most suppose."

-English poet William Cowper

Money can cost you happiness

"It is said that for money you can have everything, but you cannot. You can buy food, but not appetite; medicine, but not health; knowledge, but not wisdom; glitter, but not beauty; fun, but not joy; acquaintances, but not friends; servants, but not faithfulness; leisure, but not peace. You can have the husk of everything for money, but not the kernel." These words—by Norwegian author Arne Gaborg—sum up how I now feel about money. I used to love money, and I paid the price. It nearly took my life.

While levels of material prosperity are on the rise, so are levels of depression. We are richer than ever, but we are not happier because of it. Now I see money for what it really is. It is something that can enhance your life, but it cannot satisfy it. There are many things in this world that are worse than living from check to check. Studies have shown that money will enhance your well-being when it means avoiding poverty, but it does little more than that. In an article published in the journal *Science*, researchers found that differences in household income of more than sixty thousand dollars had little effect on daily moods. The same study found that money and job security have far less to do with how we feel than factors like deadlines on the job and sleep quality.[11] People are finding that the best things in life aren't things; they are moments. The rest is just dollars and cents.

Sadness and stress are not exclusive to the poor. National Football League (NFL) coach Andy Reid has learned this lesson the hard way. He is a millionaire, but his career has taken him away from his family. There is no doubt that this has affected his life in a negative manner. Both of his sons were recently convicted of separate drug-related felonies on the same day. While there is no proof that his job played a role in this, there will probably come a time in his life when he will wish that he made fifty thousand dollars a year and his sons were healthy and safe. Money has not bought him and his family the happiness that they probably expected.

This is just one example. Arguments about money end marriages and destroy families every day. I would much rather make forty thousand dollars a year and be a part of my brothers' lives than make a million dollars a year and lose my family. You cannot replace family and you cannot buy time. I accumulate priceless memories instead of priceless paintings. All of the nice things that I have bought can be replaced, but the memories I have of my life will stay with me for all eternity.

Yes, I have taken a hit financially, but I am richer than ever. What I had been chasing up until now were things. Material things, I realized, are immaterial. If you have what really matters—health, loving relationships, inner peace, laughter, and time—you are wealthy beyond your wildest dreams. Love is now what fuels me and feeds my soul. I have started to enjoy my life. I have been to a Yankees game. I have seen "Touchdown Jesus" at a Notre Dame

Football game. Most importantly, I have allowed myself to do nothing—which is very new to me.

If you would like to experience the same feelings, it is simpler than it seems. If you could do anything that you wanted—regardless of finances—what would you do? Brainstorm, and then find a way to make it happen. Take money out of the equation. You do not have to have a million dollars to do what brings you happiness. You might not have the resources to become an astronaut or travel the world, but you can join an astronomy club or read travel books. Face it, you may never get to play professional baseball or be in a rock band. But nothing is stopping you from joining a church softball league or learning to play an instrument with your family? These small steps could be the start of a wonderful journey that leads you as far as you want to go.

> "If there is to be any peace it will come through being, not having."
>
> -American painter Henry Miller

Money does not buy time

An armed robber once accosted comedian Jack Benny. "Your money or your life," the man exclaimed. When Benny failed to respond, his assailant repeated the demand: "What will it be; your money or your life?" At last, Benny reluctantly replied, "I'm thinking! I'm thinking!"

Do you place this much value on your money? You do if you believe that it is more valuable than your time. How you spend your time affects your life far more than how you spend your money. Your time is the single most valuable commodity on this planet—it cannot be deposited in a bank, saved in a vault, or purchased at any price. Once you have spent a second, it is gone forever. There is not enough money in the world to purchase one more minute of time. Yet you budget your finances while you spend—or waste—your time too freely.

Consider this: how often have you paid a bill with a smile on your face? Writing the check for the mortgage can sting, but it buys you and your family a month of shelter and the ability to make the memories that turn your house into a home. At the same time, you smile on payday at a job that you hate. The irony is palpable.

Many people say that they want to make a lot of money, but the material things in their life do not bring them pleasure. They do not care as much about speedboats and trust funds as they do about finding the freedom to do the things that they love. It is not necessary to have a lot of cash to have that freedom. You just have to be creative and think outside the box.

This revelation is leading to a new trend where people are starting to turn down jobs that offer a much larger salary. I am one of them. I made the conscious decision that if I make a million dollars —or go broke—I will make sure that I have the time to enjoy the trip. I no longer see the need to waste this life chasing the golden calf. I also learned very quickly that the dollar can go a lot further when you are careful about how you spend it.

> "The more you chase money, the harder it is to catch it."
>
> -Vice president of CNET networks
> Mike Tatum

Find the leak in the money bucket

Former professional golfer Doug Sanders often had difficulty with his personal finances. "I'm working as hard as I can to get my life and my cash to run out at the same time," he declared one day. "If I can just die after lunch Tuesday, everything would be perfect."

If Doug would have only known where his money was going, he might have been a lot better off. Budgeting is a crucial step in ensuring your financial safety for the present, as well as the future. Become more aware of every dollar that comes in and every dollar that goes out. Find out exactly how much it costs you to live—your fixed expenses. This will help you determine how much money you need to spend and how much money you may be wasting. It will also allow you to see how much money you could be putting to good use. Most importantly, budgeting allows you to find areas where you can tighten the belt and get a little more month out of your money.

When you are putting together your budget, make sure that you include the following items:

Home:
Rent/Mortgage: $_____
Homeowners Insurance: $_____
Telephone: $_____
Internet: $_____
Gas/Electric: $_____
Water: $_____
Garbage/Recycling: $_____
Maintenance/Repairs: $_____
Other: _____ $_____

Automobile:
Car Payment: $_____
Car Insurance: $_____
Gas: $_____
Maintenance/Repairs: $_____
Public Transportation: $_____
Other: _____ $_____

Debts:
Student Loans: $_____
Credit Cards: $_____
Child-Care Costs: $_____
Child-Support: $_____
Health-Club Membership: $_____
Other: _____ $_____
_____ $_____
_____ $_____

Food:
Supermarket: $_____

Restaurants: $_____

Carry-Out/Delivery: $_____

Other: _____ $_____

Medical expenses:
    Health Insurance: $_____
    Life Insurance: $_____
    Doctor's Visits: $_____
    Prescriptions/Vitamins: $_____
    Other: _____ $_____

Saving:
    Savings Account: $_____
    Savings Bonds: $_____
    CD's: $_____
    Other: _____ $_____
    _____ $_____

Charitable Giving:
    Church: $_____
    Non-Profit Organizations: $_____
    Other: _____ $_____
    _____ $_____

Retirement/Investments:
    401K: $_____
    IRA: $_____
    Stocks: $_____
    Other: _____ $_____

Discretionary Spending:
    Clothing: $_____
    Pet Related Costs: $_____
    Movies/Video Rental: $_____
    Books/Magazines/Newspapers: $_____
    Travel: $_____
    Other: _____ $_____

_____	$_____
_____	$_____

Total Expenses	$_____

When you are done with your budgeting for the month, you should know if you are going to run out of money before you run out of time. If your income is not enough to allow you to do the things that you need to do now and will want to do in your future, you may have to make some changes. You will have to make more money or look at ways to cut back by learning how to "under-budget" for your lifestyle.

Waste not, want not

We throw away a lot more money than we think. We think very little of spending five dollars on an espresso or a pack of cigarettes, but these purchases can really add up over a lifetime. I wanted to find out how much these types of purchases burden our pocketbooks. I followed the spending habits of ten "average" people for three months. I monitored eight of the expenditures that I deemed to be the most wasteful. I did not inquire about anything that I would consider an entertainment expense, such as movies, books, music, and dining out with family. While these types of things can get expensive if you are on a tight budget, they bring joy and meaning to your life. I would never consider that a waste.

By using these figures, I was able to make some assumptions about the amount of money we spend that could go to things that are more worthwhile.

An "average" month*:

Fast food lunch: $5 x 12 times	= $60
Cigarettes: $5 x 14 packs	= $70
"Designer" coffee: $5 x 16 times	= $80
12-pack of beer: $15 x 4	= $60
Bottle of wine: $20 x 2	= $40
Bottle of pop: $1.50 x 30	= $45
ATM Fees: $2 x 4	= $8
Bottled water: $1.50 x 20	= $30
Total:	=$393

*These figures are for a town with a very low cost of living. Adjust the figures according to your local cost of living.

I think that for many people this is a conservative estimate. Many people eat fast food more often than twelve times a month. Many others smoke more than a pack of cigarettes a day or spend hundreds of dollars a month on alcohol. It is safe to assume that there are people in this country that waste over six hundred dollars a month on wasteful purchases. That is over seven thousand dollars a year! You can imagine what that figure would become for a married couple with two kids. There is no wonder that many of us are constantly strapped for cash.

Imagine how much fatter your bank account—and skinnier your waistline—could be if you cut these things out of your life. You could do so many good things with this money. You could pay off your credit cards, support a worthy charity, or spend it on a family vacation. All of these things would bring more joy to your life than a bacon cheeseburger and a smoke.

Ten Tips for under-budgeting

1. Cut up your credit cards immediately. If you cannot pay cash for it, you cannot afford it.
2. Stay out of the drive thru. Prepare your own food whenever you can. Not only will you save money, you will also improve your health.
3. Buy used vehicles. Let someone else pay for the depreciation on your car. Many pre-owned vehicles are in great shape and come with a warranty.
4. Enjoy the fun things in life that are inexpensive or free. Go to the library. Take your family to an outdoor festival. Go to the park.
5. Spend less at the grocery store. Stay away from prepackaged foods and expensive beverages.
6. Don't overdo the holidays. Teach your family the real reason for the season. The holidays are about being thankful for what we have, not for focusing on what we want.
7. Keep your bank balance on you at all times. Every time that you make a purchase, deduct it from your account. It is much harder to waste money when you have to see it drain from your account immediately.
8. Use energy-efficient appliances and lighting. Use your heating and cooling systems sparingly. Turn the lights off and the thermostat down whenever you leave the house. These are great tips to help the environment and your pocketbook at the same time.
9. Use the internet to look for good deals on all of your major purchases. Websites like Overstock.com and eBay.com can save you a considerable amount of money, as long as you know where to look.
10. Vacation closer to home, or in the off-season. It will save you hundreds—if not thousands—of dollars, and you will not have to fight the crowds.

Life Lessons:

- Put money in its place. The sooner you realize that there are things more valuable than money, the better off you will be. Constantly remind yourself that your family, your health, and your happiness are much more important than stocks and bonds. The best things in life are not things at all.
- It's not what you make; it's what you keep. You may have to tighten the purse strings now in order to secure your finances for the future. Paying down your credit cards, student loans, and mortgage now can save you tens of thousands of dollars later.
- Get a handle on your finances. The better you budget your money, the less you will have to stress about it.
- Learn to enjoy yourself without having to spend a lot of money. If you need an incentive, remind yourself that every dollar you save leads you to an earlier retirement or a better future for your children.

Part II: Love Your Life

"If people concentrated on the really important things in life, there'd be a shortage of fishing poles."

-British middle-distance runner
Doug Larson

Chapter 6

Keep the Corvette in the Garage: Avoiding the Midlife Crisis

> "I try to take one day at a time, but sometimes several days attack me at once."
>
> -Artist and writer Jennifer Yane

Well into his sunset years, Jack Benny would tell his friends that he was thirty-nine years old. Frank Sinatra found the perfect gift to give Benny for his eightieth birthday: two copies of the book *Life Begins at 40*.

You probably have the same mental picture as I do when you think of a midlife crisis—the forty-five year old man with a cherry-red convertible and a bad toupee. These superficial lifestyle changes are only the tip of the iceberg. A midlife crisis can be much more damaging. They destroy lives every day, and it has the potential to do the same to you if you do not know how to deal with it.

A search for meaning

Millions of people will experience the symptoms of a midlife crisis at some point during their life. They are common during midlife—hence the name—because your middle age years are a time of reflection and reassessment. However, research shows that more than half of all self-reported midlife crises occur before the age of forty or after the age of fifty.[12] These problems can strike at any age.

The Midlife crisis is an umbrella term that clumps together three or four different—but related—issues, ranging from clinical depression to a casual reassessment of your life. The textbook definition is a severe psychological crisis brought on by the realization that one's time is running out. More commonly, though, it is a term used to describe self-doubt brought on by an obsession with mortality and the loss of youth.

If you do not understand the process, it can feel like a serious dilemma. People going through a midlife crisis suffer a variety of symptoms and exhibit disparate behaviors. The result may be a desire to make significant changes in a career, a marriage, or other core aspects of day-to-day life.

The causes of a midlife crisis differ between men and women, with work issues being a more likely spark in men. Women's midlife crises are more likely to be brought on by family events or marital problems. Male or female, they are usually triggered by aging, or aging in combination with changes, problems, or regrets over:

- Physical changes associated with aging
- Job loss or a stalled career
- Marriage or divorce
- Maturation of children
- Aging or death of parents
- Questioning your life path
- Debt or other financial worries

If you are going through a midlife crisis, you will experience a wide range of feelings. The suffering is built around a deep unhappiness with your life so far, and confusion about where it is going. The search for meaning can make you feel discontent with your life and the material possessions in it. Sufferers develop a deep sense of remorse for unaccomplished goals. Everything in their life feels like a never-ending series of demands on them. They feel trapped.

The cornerstone of a midlife crisis is a feeling that time is running out. Sufferers spend an excessive amount of time reminiscing about their youth—a better period in their life. They become restless, and they develop a sudden obsession with achieving that feeling of youthfulness once again.

These newfound emotions make them feel adventurous. They feel like they need to do something completely different—to change for the sake of change. The midlife crisis is famous for several behavioral changes, including increased attention to physical appearance, and conspicuous consumption—acquisition of items such as clothing, sports cars, jewelry, and motorcycles. These feelings may lead you to believe that a toupee, a new Porsche, and an exciting new job as a stuntman make perfect sense. These radical lifestyle changes will almost always be regretted in the future.

It commonly hits men harder than women. Men have a lot more trouble dealing with change. Wall street journal columnist Sue Shellenbarger put it best when she wrote, "Women undergo bigger changes than men in middle age, but they have a more positive attitude about their prospects in life." Women seem more capable of dealing with these behavioral issues before they transform into a psychological crisis.

Some of the more serious psychological issues that can develop include:

- Sleeping more, loss of appetite, and general malaise—signs of depression
- A need to spend more time alone or with certain peers
- Increase in alcohol consumption or drug use
- Changes in sexual relationships; a desire to find new sexual partners

---

"The midlife crisis is a cliché—until you have one."

- *Wall Street Journal* contributor Sue Shellenbarger

The truth will set you free

To deal with something, you must first understand it. There are many myths and misconceptions surrounding the midlife crisis, and many of these popular notions are simply not true.

For starters, the midlife crisis has a lot more to do with life circumstances than age. While commonly called a midlife crisis, these changes are often just crises that happen in midlife. These upheavals are not unique to middle age and are not age-related. In one study, less than 10% of midlife crisis sufferers had psychological complaints due to their age or aging.[13] Elaine Wethingon—a professor of sociology at Cornell University—said that, "When you look more closely, sufferers are saying that it is a crisis that occurred at forty years old rather than a crisis that was caused by the fact that they are forty."

These behavioral changes and psychological problems are not unique to middle aged people. The quarter-life crisis—similar symptoms at a younger age—is becoming more and more common. Our increasing pace of life causes life to go by faster than ever, which makes us wonder where all the time has gone at an earlier age. People in their twenties and thirties are more concerned with making sense of their life than they were a generation ago. Life is so hectic that a midlife crisis can strike at any moment.

The final misconception that people have about the midlife crisis is whether or not they actually have one. They are far less common than people think. The popular belief that practically everyone goes through a midlife crisis provides cover for people who want to do these things anyway. Sometimes it is not a crisis; it is an excuse.

Dr. O's action-steps to manage a midlife crisis

Sometimes a midlife crisis works out for the better. Sometimes a period of reassessment is just what you need to light a fire in your life. Just make sure that you are doing it for the right reason. Restless feelings and radical life choices can force people to start life over at square one. You can use the following steps to keep yourself from suffering the same fate.

1. Face it head on

We have an amazing capacity to ignore important warning signs. Disregarding the background hum of unease in our lives is all too easy to do. Don't learn to live with a midlife crisis. By sticking your head in the sand, you may be ignoring important information.

The most constructive way to deal with these issues is to embrace them. Without properly identifying what is wrong, there is no way to fix it. Embrace your problems as a chance to reassess your life and make positive changes. If the path you are on at midlife is making you so uncomfortable, change. Just be sure that you are making constructive changes, not destructive ones.

2. Plan your attack

We are hard-wired to think that if we are suffering, there must be a problem. And, if there is a problem, it should be figured out, given a name, and quickly resolved.

People in painful situations often believe that if they make changes to their life, the hurting will stop. They quit their jobs, leave their marriages, and change their appearance, all in an attempt to see if they can make the pain go away. It might. It might not. Either way, it is a temporary solution.

Don't throw away the security that you have built up in your life by reacting too quickly. You may find yourself making poor or irrational decisions as you attempt to come to terms with your life. Decisions that could haunt you forever.

You have the time necessary to evaluate what is going on before you act. The clock will continue to tick; that is what clocks do. Things are okay as long as there is a tomorrow on the calendar.

3. Do not numb it

I used to drink myself blind to keep from seeing how much I hated my life.

We do things like this to make our problems go away—or at least numb them. We abuse drugs, alcohol, sex, television, and the internet to get some form of short-term relief.

Other normal activities taken to an extreme to numb the pain include gambling, excessive shopping, and buying new "toys". Any one of these pursuits or activities is considered normal and can be beneficial. However, they are unhealthy if taken to the extreme for the sole purpose of temporary happiness.

4. Take it seriously

A midlife crisis is the tragic expression of an unmet need. It is a serious problem, and it needs to be handled as such. Everyone will deal with this type of situation in their own way. Do not try to copy what has worked for someone else. In the words of Theodore Roosevelt: "Do what you can, with what you have, where you are."

Once you admit to yourself that you have a serious problem, you can find a workable solution. Remember that what you are dealing with is how much you love your life and value your future. Do not try to make it a laughing matter. Treat it like you would any other health problem. Get a complete physical, watch what you eat, and get a little exercise. If you are feeling overwhelmed, take mental health days to get your mind right. Find ways to love yourself for who you are, not who you wish you could be. In the scope of forever, loving yourself—flaws and all—is all that matters.

5. Do not take it on alone

I have a new feeling of restlessness, but it is a positive one. I feel like I have to increase awareness about the problems that plague our society—stress, midlife crisis, burnout, etc.—that many people try to deal with on their own. To make society-wide changes we must first understand that these problems are common, normal, and manageable. Awareness leads to understanding, and understanding leads to solutions.

Do not try to go at it alone. Explain your situation to family, friends, and understanding coworkers. Use the resources that are at your disposal (See resource directory at the end of the book). Inquire at your employers Human Resource Department about any available assistance. These steps will aid in your recovery and put you back on the right path.

If these strategies are not helping you make the progress that you desire, seek professional assistance. Find a psychologists, psychiatrists, or career counselor that specializes in dealing with your particular dilemma. Speak to someone with counseling experience at your church or parish. Consider marriage or family counseling if your crisis is harming your personal relationships. Whatever you do, do something, and do it now.

Life Lessons:

- A midlife crisis can lead to issues ranging from a reassessment of one's life to severe depression. The cornerstone of a true midlife crisis is a feeling that the sand is running out of the hourglass. It can be much more serious than a new wardrobe and a trophy wife. While many people laugh it off as a cliché, it can destroy years of hard work and achievement in a matter of days.
- A midlife crisis can feel very uncomfortable, and the need to achieve a feeling of youthfulness causes people to make radical lifestyle changes that will be regretted in the future. These behavioral changes include an obsession with physical appearance and the purchase of items like sports cars, motorcycles, and a spray tan.
- While commonly called a midlife crisis, these changes are often just crises that happen in midlife. Life is so hectic that a midlife crisis can strike at any moment. These feelings are not unique to middle age and are not age-related. It is usually a crisis that occurs as we turn fifty years old rather than a crisis that occurs because we turned fifty years old.

Chapter 7

Enough Is Enough: Finding Work-Life Balance

"Men for the sake of getting a living forget to live."

-American gender theorist Margaret Fuller

I used to see life as a series of items on a to-do list. My days were nothing more than a string of meetings to attend, tasks to finish, and activities to complete. My schedule was so full that I could barely breathe. Every minute seemed to matter, but the minutes I had were never enough. My life was a mess.

I was not alone. Americans have the most severe problem with work-life balance in the world. According to the Center for Work and the Family, we spend 163 more hours a year on the job than we did twenty years ago.[14] That is the equivalent of an extra month of work every year.

We work too much. We bring work home with us. We don't take enough vacation time. We don't get enough sleep. We let our work invade our playtime. We have lost control.

Waging a war for your time

Life is one continuous rush. We cram our days with activities, thinking that each one is as important as the next. Keeping our bosses happy hurts our home life. Meeting the needs of our families causes our work to suffer. The balancing act between the two is not easy.

The traditional family with a male breadwinner and a wife at home no longer fits into today's society. Many parents with children have an extra ten to fifteen hours per week of work—chauffeur, chef, counselor—once they get home from their job. Working moms are preoccupied with work while at home. Working dads are asked to work evenings and weekends. Even though we work more than ever, we cannot get enough of it done. This demonstrates the pressure employees are under to be available to the office, despite responsibilities or plans away from work.

Economics Professor Andrew Oswald found that 85% of workers want more time with their family.[15] The same study found that 37% of working dads would consider taking a new job with less pay if it offered a better work-life balance.[16] Another study of over thirty thousand people found that 80% were unhappy with their work-life balance.[17] It is becoming more and more obvious that these problems are affecting millions of us.

The solution is to create a better work-life balance. If you budget properly, schedule your life properly, and learn to say no, you can keep from giving too much of yourself. You do not have to be overworked and "under-played". You can find a balance between your work and the rest of your life. You can get eight hours of sleep at night and still spend quality time with your family. Simply put, you can work to live, instead of living to work.

Technology: savior or culprit

Harold Wilson, English Prime Minister in 1964, proclaimed that jobholders would be enjoying fifteen-hour workweeks by the year 2000 thanks to the advancement of technology. Fast forward to today and white-collar employees in Great Britain are working ten hours a week longer than at the time Wilson made his prediction.[18] Where is all of the time that we save? When do we get it back? When is enough, enough?

As technology transforms the workplace—accelerating the pace of activities, increasing productivity demands, and blurring the line between work and play—workers are growing increasingly unhappy with their jobs. All of this amazing technology was supposed to free us, but it has made us slaves. Technology has made it virtually impossible to unplug from your work. It forces us to do more work in less time, not have more free time to ourselves. Our astonishing high-speed life has made our attention span so short that we do not experience what we are doing. We are busy moving on to the next thing.

A lack of productivity

NATO Secretary General Joseph Luns was once asked how many people worked at NATO. His reply was, "About half of them."

People are working longer, but are they working smarter? Our high-speed technology has made our attention span so short that we do not have the patience to concentrate on our work. We appear busy because we rush everywhere, but in reality, we waste a lot of time energy. We cannot get everything done because we are traveling in circles. According to the Microsoft Office Personal Productivity Challenge, Americans work an average of forty-five hours a week. Sixteen of these hours were reported to be unproductive. 66% of respondents feel that this unproductive use of time is a major reason that they do not have a balance between their work and the rest of their life.[19] It is becoming evident that getting the most out of people does not mean getting the best out of them.

Some of the drains on our productivity at work include:
- Surfing the internet
- E-mail
- Personal business: phone calls, paying bills online
- Socializing with co-workers
- Staring off into space
- Computer games
- Running errands: dry cleaning, hair appointments

No wonder we have to go to work early, stay late, and bring work home on the weekends. If we were to minimize these productivity parasites, perhaps we wouldn't need to. We could become a much more productive workforce if we worked fewer hours and fewer days, and went to work happy and refreshed at a job that we truly care about.

"Slow down and enjoy life. It's not only the scenery you miss by going too fast—you also miss the sense of where you are going and why."

-Actor Eddie Cantor

A model of balance

It is awe-inspiring to watch an individual perform at the highest level of their profession while maintaining balance in their life. There is no better example of this ability than former NFL head coach Tony Dungy.

Tony Dungy led the Indianapolis Colts to a Super Bowl championship in 2007, becoming the first African-American coach to do so. He is one of only three people to win the Super Bowl as both a player and a coach.[20] Above all of this, what sets him apart is that he has accomplished so much in his career without sacrificing his family and his values in the process.

Dungy keeps his family first, and he can still coach a team to a Super Bowl win. When asked about this, he said: "For your faith to be more important than your job, for your family to be more important than your job, we all know that's the way it should be, but we're afraid to say that sometimes. I'm not afraid to say it." He has always prioritized his role as a husband and father ahead of his job, and he encourages his players and staff to do the same. By all accounts, Tony Dungy leads the most balanced life of any head coach in the history of the NFL. "He is faith, family, football, in that order and with no exceptions," says former Kansas City Chiefs coach Herm Edwards.

Many of his peers are less successful, even though they sleep on a cot in their office and work eighteen hours a day.[21] At the same time, Dungy takes his children to school in the morning and leaves work early whenever he can. No first in, last to leave stuff with him. His primary advice for parents—fathers in particular—is to just be around and be available to your children.

Dungy has earned widespread admiration due to his strong convictions and his high standards of ethics and behavior. Perhaps this is part of the reason that he is so well respected. Former Colts player Edgerrin James said, "Whether I'm playing on his team or not, he's forever my coach." Another former player, Warren Sapp, called Dungy "the greatest man I've ever met in my life."

Dungy is a devout Christian and at one point considered leaving football for the prison ministry. He takes his position as a role model very important. He regularly speaks out about the importance of being a good father, and he makes the time to be involved in many charitable organizations, including the Fellowship of Christian Athletes (FCA), Athletes in Action, Big Brothers Big Sisters, and Family First.[22]

Tony Dungy's book, *Quiet Strength*, has been called an inspiring message of hope to people concerned about what their future holds. He is trying to spread his family first message to millions of people, starting with his inner circle. Assistant coach Jim Caldwell said, "He sets a tone. I think you'll find that every one of us has become a better father being around him." We would all be lucky to have a boss like this.

Workaholics

At its peak, Jim Cramer's finance firm controlled more than four hundred million dollars. When things went badly, he would sweat and curse, shriek at colleagues and brokers, smash telephone receivers on the trading desk, and throw computer monitors to the ground, sending black smoke curling upward in the office.

In his aptly-entitled *Confessions of a Street Addict*,[23] Cramer admits that he talked stocks with friends hours after his mother's death and that he took a call from his research director in the delivery room—just as his wife was giving birth.

Workaholics become dependent on their work to give them an identity—a sense of who they are—and to gain a positive sense of themselves. They dive into their work as an escape or a psychological safe haven. Work becomes such an addiction that they struggle to break the grasp that it holds on them.

Workaholism is a disease that has millions of unfortunate casualties. Workers that let their job consume their life. Spouses whose only mistake was to fall in love with someone who cares more about their work than their personal relationships. Children who blame themselves even though the only thing that they did wrong was to try to get some love and affection from their parent. Workaholics leave a trail of broken promises and broken hearts wherever they go.

Do not get me wrong, many workaholics are inherently good people. They just do not understand what is going wrong, so they cannot do what they need to do to fix it. If they see the warning signs and use the available resources, perhaps it isn't too late for a happily ever after kind of life.

"You don't have to die in order to make a living."

-Canadian cartoonist Lynn Johnston

How do you know if you are a workaholic?
1. You have an unhealthy emotional attachment to your job:
   - Do you like to talk about work after hours?
   - Do you think about your work while driving, falling asleep, or when others are talking?
   - Do you get more excited about your work than your social life or hobbies?
2. You are worried that your employer will suffer in your absence:
   - Do you take on extra work because you are concerned that it will not otherwise get done?
   - Do you take complete responsibility for the outcome of your work efforts?

- Do you take work with you to bed? On weekends? On vacation?
3. You get an excessive amount of physical enjoyment from your work:
    - Do you believe that it is okay to work long hours if you love what you do?
    - Do you get impatient with people who have other priorities besides work?
    - Do you get irritated when people ask you to stop doing your work in order to do something else?
4. You let fear control your relationship with work:
    - Are you afraid that if you do not work hard you will lose your job?
    - Does an intense fear of failure drive you?
    - Do you believe that more money will solve all the problems in your life?
5. You continue to work compulsively even though it is hurting the rest of your life:
    - Have your long hours hurt your family or other relationships?
    - Have your family and friends given up on expecting you on time?
    - Do you work during meals or recreational activities?

If you answered yes to four or more of these questions, there is a good chance that your work life has taken on a life of its own. The good news is that workaholism can be treated just like any other disease. Now is the time to break free from the shackles that bind you to a job that cares a lot less about you than you care about it.

The workaholism cure

1. Join Workaholics Anonymous

Workaholics Anonymous is the organization created to help people deal with the desire to stop working compulsively. Workaholics Anonymous has one primary purpose—to carry its message to the workaholic who still suffers. The only requirement for membership is a desire to stop working compulsively.24 Visit www.Workaholics-Anonymous.org for resource materials and more information about how to join.

2. Prioritize your life

Think before accepting any commitments that will affect your work, family, or time. Decide which are the most important things to do first. Sometimes that may mean doing nothing. You are more effective by being more selective. Stay as flexible as you can. Do not add a new activity without eliminating something else from your schedule that takes as much time.

3. Schedule time for play

CBS President Fred Silverman was once asked by a friend whether he planned to go home for the Yom Kippur holiday. On which day did Yom Kippur fall, Silverman wondered. "Wednesday," said the friend. "Wednesday!" cried Silverman. "You mean they've scheduled Yom Kippur opposite *Charlie's Angels*!"

You need to refuse to let yourself work constantly to keep from becoming this crazed about your job. Make sure that your life is full—yet under-scheduled. Use the tips in this book to balance your workload with your family, your friends, and your God. The more you take it easy, the more you can accomplish. Rest is the best reward that you can give yourself. Listen to your body and obey its signals. When it is time for rest, drop everything and unwind.

4. Work to live, don't live to work

You may not here this often enough, but you are perfect just the way that you are. God broke the mold when He made you. You will never be happy with your life or your career until you love yourself no matter what.

Try to live each moment like it is a precious gift. Your maker does not want you to work your life away. Work is meant to be the means to an end. The end is supposed to be a happy, fulfilled life.

Life Lessons:

- Americans have the most severe problem with work-life balance in the world. We have lost control of our lives. Technology has connected us to our work like no other time in history. It has made it virtually impossible to hide from our jobs.
- Millions of workers want more time with their family. The solution is to create a work-life balance that will allow you eight hours to work, eight hours to sleep, and eight hours for yourself and your family. If you budget properly, schedule your life properly, and learn to say no, you can make this life a reality.
- We are a very hardworking people, but we waste a tremendous amount of time on the job. The average American worker spends at least 35% of their workweek on unproductive tasks that sap their energy and test their patience.[25] We appear busier than employees in other nations do, but it does not show up in our productivity.
- Workaholics become dependent on their work to give them an identity and to gain a positive sense of themselves. Their work is an escape and a safe place. Work becomes such an addiction that they struggle to break the grasp that it holds on them. The good news is that workaholism can be beaten just like any other addiction.

Chapter 8

Later Is Now: Your Ticket to a Happy Life

"There are two great days in a person's life—the day we are born and the day we discover why."

-Theologian William Barclay

I love the fact that we live in a world where a blind man can climb Mount Everest and an 84-year-old woman can run the Ironman triathlon. You don't have to settle for a cookie-cutter life. You can do anything that your heart desires as long as you stop making excuses and start creating your own future. You have to grow old; your dreams do not.

When you realize how much more you can do, and how much more you can contribute to this world, you will find true happiness. It is never too late to transform your ordinary life into something extraordinary. You are going to be fifty anyway, why not be a happy and fulfilled fifty. You can create a life that allows you to build on your gifts and experiences, so that when you look back and ask, "What have I done with my life?" You can say "Everything that I wanted."

If not now, when?

All too often, we miss the most important events in our lives. We don't recognize the special moments that are happening while we are busy making other plans. Some of us are living in the past. Most of us are living in the future. Very few of us are cherishing the present. It is crucial that you see the present as the gift that it is.

The reality is that your life could end today, or the world could end tomorrow. You will be much happier if you learn to live your life like a choose-your-own adventure book instead of a novel that you cannot wait to get to the end of. Live your life like there's no tomorrow in case you are right.

Why do you worry so much about a future that you have no true control over? There is nothing to rush off to that can offer you anything more than this very moment. Today's urgent problems will soon become tomorrow's distant memories. That is the habit of all problems. They seem unbearable at the time, but when you look back on them from a better vantage point, you realize one of two things. Either the problem was not as bad as you thought at the time, or it was actually a blessing in disguise. How many times has an unexpected circumstance in your life led you to a better place? Imagine the fear and worry that a young woman has when she first gets the news that she is unexpectedly pregnant. Fast-forward ten years, and she wouldn't trade her child for anything in the world. Compare your problems today with the problems you had ten years ago. You will see that they took more time and energy than they ever deserved.

As I began to see this, I started to make the quality of each day matter more than getting things done. I learned to live in the moment and enjoy the very process of living. Worrying less about the future will free up your creative energy and passion. Instead of racing through life, try taking the scenic route. You will still get to your destination, but you can make time to see the sites and enjoy the ride.

Do not hurry away from this moment; it has taken a lifetime to get here. Everything you need is right here, right now. Do not let your happiness hinge on the future. If you do, you will miss all of the great things that are happening in the present.

> "Nothing is as far away as one minute ago."
>
> -Comic creator Jef Mallett

Your new life is waiting

The main reason that people do not get what they want out of life is that they cannot figure out what it is that they are looking for. I want to help you get where you want to go, but only you can decide where that is. Begin by making a list of the things that you want to accomplish and the people that you want to impact before you die. Ask yourself what the most passionate life you can create would look like. Give yourself the freedom to dream, but be realistic. Use the following questions as a jumping off point.

> "He who has a why to live can bear almost any how."
>
> -German philosopher Friedrich Nietzsche

Personal:
- If people would say one thing about you, what would you like that to be?

_____

_____

_____

- What do you want to be remembered for?

_____

_____

_____

- Do you want to make money or memories?

_____

_____

_____

- What do you want to learn, to have, to experience?

_____

_____

_____

Family:
- Do you want to be married?

_____

_____

- How many children do you want to have?

_____

_____

- How close do you want to be with your parents and/or siblings?

_____

_____

- What do you want to teach your family through your living?

_____

_____

_____

Friends:
- Why will people be thankful to have known you?

_____

_____

- How many close friends would you like to have?

_____

_____

- How would you like to spend your time with your friends?

_____

_____

- What makes someone the type of person that you would like to call a friend?

_____

_____

_____

Work:
- What type of career would give you the most happiness?

_____

_____

- How many hours and days a week do you want to work?

_____

_____

- Do you want to work from home some or all of the time?

_____

_____

- Do you want to be home with your family in the morning and/or at the dinner table at night?

_____

_____

_____

Causes:
- How are you going to make this a better world for your children and grandchildren?

_____

_____

- Do you enjoy spending time at church meetings, or volunteering your time?

_____

_____

_____

- Are you passionate about a cause greater than yourself? God? The environment? Human rights?

_____

_____

_____

- Do you want to help children, the elderly, or people with mental or physical handicaps?

_____

_____

_____

Places:
- Where do you want to live?

_____

_____

- Do you have a special place where you want to retire?

_____

_____

- Do you have a list of ten or twenty places that you want to visit before you die?

_____

_____

- Is there a place where you like to spend your leisure time? A place that helps you unwind?

_____

_____

_____

Things:
- Do you want to create a piece of art, restore a classic car, or start a stamp collection?

_____

_____

_____

- Do you enjoy home improvements or landscaping?

_____

_____

_____

- Do you want to own a boat, a motorcycle, or a vacation timeshare?

_____

_____

_____

- Do you have a hobby that has always made you happy?

_____

_____

_____

A note before you begin. Your goals and aspirations are constantly going to grow and evolve over time. Your to-do list should change to reflect that. You should complete this exercise at least once every five years. I personally use this exercise every December. I use it to gauge my progress over the past year while isolating my focus on the things that I have deemed important for the next year.

"If we take care of the moments, the years will take care of themselves."

-Publisher Malcolm Forbes

Now get a life

Once you have answered these questions, you now have the only to-do list that you will ever need. Your list should read as the outline of your autobiography. You can begin to create the road map for the rest of your life.

The next step is to start living the life that takes you there. What will you have to do in order to live the kind of life that you will feel great about? Get your creative juices flowing—brainstorm—and create action steps that will lead you to the completion of this list.

Try to think of at least two action steps for every item. For example, one of the items on my list is to have a great relationship with my youngest brother Tanner. The list that I created to ensure that would happen is as follows:

1. Talk to him at least four times a week.
2. Attend at least 80% of his school functions and sporting events.
3. Find two hobbies that we can share together.

Once you have all of your action steps in place, you can see if the way you are living your life is in line with what you truly want to accomplish. You can give more meaning to your day-to-day life by making each moment a part of something bigger. Whenever you need to decide between two people, places, or things, you can choose the one that will help you accomplish something in your life plan. This will allow you to make sure that everything you are doing is worthy of your valuable time.

Assume that one of your life goals is to climb Mount Everest. Would it be better for you to watch a documentary on mountain climbing or a documentary on how cheese is made? Would it be better to spend your vacation on a hiking trip or at Disneyland? Should you use your free time to exercise or read? Knowing where you are going with your life will keep you on track, and it will minimize the amount of time you waste on nonproductive activities.

A friend of mine followed this advice, and it paid huge dividends in his life. He created the life that he wanted by having a plan and a timetable that would make him happy. He started out as an avid auto-racing fan, and ended up becoming a member of an IndyCar pit crew in a matter of months. He turned his dream into a reality by following his blueprint religiously. Rather than watching the races on television, he went to them whenever possible. While his friends were drinking and meeting girls, he was passing out resumes and meeting as many influential people as possible. His big break came when he met the limo driver for the owner of a racing team. He was soon on his way to living his dream. Some people might chalk this story up to dumb luck, but I say that he made his own luck. Chance favors the prepared mind. Never underestimate the power of a well thought out plan, mixed with persistence and a positive attitude.

> "The person born with a talent they are meant to use will find their greatest happiness in using it."
>
> -German author
> Johann Wolfgang Von Goethe

Addition + subtraction = multiplication

The key to happiness is more than adding good things to your life. In order to accomplish more positive things in your life you are going to have to trim the fat. You can find the time to do what is important in your life by eliminating the things that are a waste. When you add positive things to your life while subtracting things that are holding you back, you will multiply your happiness exponentially.

Think of how Michelangelo felt about the creation of his sculptures. He felt like his statues were waiting for him in the stone. They started as a block of granite until he chiseled away the excess. What was left was a piece of art. Michelangelo did not have to add anything; he only took away what was interfering with the beauty that was already there. Finding the things in your life that you will have to chisel away to make this new life a reality is a crucial step.

You may also have to turn your weaknesses into your strengths to accomplish your new goals. You may have mental, emotional, physical, or social barriers to break through to make yourself the person that you aspire to be. If you can do this, you can multiply the effect of every other positive change you make in your life.

Four of the weaknesses that you will need to overcome include:

1. Self-worth issues

We have been taught to look outward to define ourselves and give us a feeling of worth. We have an unhealthy need to be better than our peers. We are validated by being smarter than, richer than, prettier than, or more talented than our co-workers and neighbors. Problems arise when we find ourselves not measuring up to society's criteria for worth. We suffer serious consequences, and we hate ourselves for our flaws—for being human.

Self-worth is how you see yourself in relation to others. It is frequently based on your feelings of worth in terms of your achievements, status, bank account, or looks. But, looks fade, trophies lose their shine, and money disappears. You can have all of the money, property, and prestige in the world, but if you are not at peace with yourself, none of it will make you happy. You can only find inner peace if you are true to yourself. You can value yourself on the inside no matter what happens.

Five ways to improve your self-worth

1. Begin to treat yourself as a worthwhile person. Forgive yourself for your flaws, and accept yourself as worthy of love and happiness.
2. Separate your identity from your position in life. Get your self-worth from things like service to humanity or helping other people find happiness.
3. List things that you like about yourself—including your appearance, personality, and skills. Remind yourself of how great you already are.
4. Make positive changes. Get a manicure, color your hair, and buy a new outfit. Do the things that make you feel good about yourself.
5. Ask for support from friends and family. Have them remind you why they love you. Be sure to return the favor.

2. Self-esteem issues

Healthy self-esteem is feeling deserving of happiness. Our self-esteem develops and evolves as we build an image of ourselves through our experiences. Our childhood experiences play a particularly large role in the shaping of our basic self-esteem.

Your self-esteem is more than the normal ups and downs associated with life. For people with poor self-esteem, these mood swings can drastically alter their perceptions and choices. Low self-esteem can have devastating consequences. It creates a downward spiral of anxiety, stress, and loneliness. These people rely on positive experiences to counteract the negative feelings that plague them. They often turn to sex, drugs, alcohol, or gambling for pleasure and validation. If they do not continue to get this positive stimulation, they can feel miserable, which in turn can lead to a state of depression.

The US Center for Disease Control and Prevention (CDC) reported that there were 118 million prescriptions for antidepressants in 2005, more than any other prescription drug.[26] More than blood pressure medication. More than cholesterol lowering drugs. Even more than the little blue erectile dysfunction pills that we are constantly forced to hear about. The CDC also reported that the use of antidepressants nearly tripled from 1988 to 2000.[27] Many experts believe that these drugs are still under-prescribed and that the problem is even worse than reported.

What would it do to your self-esteem if you lost all of your money? What if you gained fifty pounds; or lost your hair? If you lost your job title, would you lose your sense of self? If your self-esteem is wrapped up in these external outcomes, you will be setting yourself up for failure when the pendulum swings the other way. You need to find a way to keep your self-esteem separate from your day-to-day circumstances.

Five ways to improve your self-esteem

1. Accept and value yourself unconditionally. Realize that you are just the way that God made you.
2. Realistically acknowledge your strengths and limitations. Make a list of all the things that you are good at, whether it is playing a musical instrument or knitting a sweater. Constantly remind yourself that you are an expert at many things.
3. Reward yourself for your accomplishments, big or small. Compliment yourself for the good things that you do. Treat yourself to fun and relaxing activities.
4. Take classes or try out new activities to increase your sense of competence. If you want to be better at something, learn more about it. If you discover that you are not good at it,

you have two choices. Either you can move on to something different, or you can enjoy the journey by concentrating on the activity instead of the results.

5. If weight is an issue, focus on being healthy instead of being skinny. There are many unhealthy skinny people. Do not sacrifice your health for the sake of a smaller dress size. Exercise, eat in moderation, and burn more calories than you eat, but do not worry about it forever. Do not hate yourself for being you.

3. Lack of education

Maybe you feel like you need more education to create a better life. This could come in the form of a traditional education, on-the-job training, or home study courses. The good news is that it is easier than ever to go back to school. Online classes and non-traditional education programs have made these types of changes more of a reality and a possibility. My brother Rick completed a degree program for working adults that allowed him to get his bachelor's degree in sixteen months by going to school one night a week. There is now no excuse to lack the education that you want or need.

Success is a byproduct of skill, circumstance, and luck. While you cannot get lucky all of the time, you can keep the lack of an education from holding you back. An education can take you from where you are to where you want to be.

Going back to school does not have to be complicated or scary. Start by taking something that interests you. You never know where it will lead. College is more about learning how to learn—and think—than any specific subject matter. That is why so many employers want you to have a college degree but they do not really care what degree you have.

Being educated and knowledgeable can have some profound effects on your life, as well as your pocketbook. Take engineer Charles Steinmetz for example. He was once called out of retirement by General Electric to help them locate a problem in an intricate system of complex machines. Having spent some time tinkering with and testing various parts of the system, he finally placed a chalk-marked 'X' on a small component in one machine. GE's engineers promptly examined the component, and were amazed to find the defect in the precise location of Steinmetz's mark. Some time later, GE received an invoice from Steinmetz for $10,000 dollars. They protested the bill and challenged him to itemize it. Steinmetz did so: "Making one chalk mark: $1 dollar," he wrote. "Knowing where to place it: $9,999 dollars."

The effect that an education can have on your future happiness is discussed in further detail in Chapter 12.

4. Fear

Activities like skydiving remind us that fear is relative. Some people love it. Others wonder why you would jump out of a perfectly good plane. One person's fear is another person's joy. The only difference is in the perception.

There is nothing wrong with fear. Fear can keep you out of dangerous situations and keep you alive. Fear is only an issue if it stands directly between where you are and where you want to be. For example, I am deathly afraid of bats due to a childhood incident. I would rather take my chances with an angry gorilla than a "flying rat". If I wanted to become a park ranger or a zoologist, I would have to address it. However, I do not, so I never plan to face that fear. I plan to avoid bats whenever possible. I also plan to keep an exterminator and animal control on speed dial for as long as I live.

The biggest weakness that I had to overcome to alter my life course was my fear of public speaking. I would get physically ill when I knew that I had to give a speech in high school. I tried to take a public speaking class in college, but I dropped out of the class after the first day. As Jerry Seinfeld's story goes, I would rather have been the one in the casket at a funeral than the one giving the eulogy.

I knew that I had to remedy this situation if I was going to achieve the goals that I had set for my life. I joined Toastmaster's International, a leadership and communications skills organization. I volunteered to give community education classes as part of my clinical internship. I tried to strike up a conversation with at least one stranger every day. I pushed myself until I was no longer afraid. I went from being afraid to speak to a group of three people to thriving on giving talks to a thousand people or more. The rest is history.

I can only imagine how different my personal and professional life would be if I had not turned this weakness into a strength. My improved ability to communicate has allowed me to become a successful doctor, a professor, a coveted public speaker, and an author. It has also transformed my personal life. I used to be a wallflower, now I enter any situation with a newfound confidence. Changing my weaknesses into my strengths has allowed me to accomplish things that I never dreamt possible.

Life Lessons:

- Stop making excuses and create your future. Envision a life that you would enjoy living, and then make it happen.
- Create your road map to a happy life by deciding what you want to accomplish, and create the plan that will lead you to your destination.
- Treat yourself as a worthwhile person. Accept and value yourself by acknowledging your strengths and forgiving your limitations.
- If there is something in your life that is holding you back, do everything that you can to face it head on. Your future will never be brighter if you can turn your weaknesses into strengths.

Chapter 9

Live Like a Kid Again: Squeezing Every Ounce Out of Your Life

> "I am careful not to confuse excellence with perfection. Excellence, I can reach for; perfection is God's business."
>
> -Actor Michael J. Fox

Someone once remarked upon the huge number of failures that Thomas Edison had racked up in his quest for a practical storage battery—fifty thousand failed experiments before finally achieving any results. "Results?" the inventor replied. "Why, I have gotten a lot of results. I know fifty thousand things that won't work!"

The only place that the past exists is in your mind. Your past mistakes cannot haunt you, only you can haunt yourself with them. Look at your mistakes as something that you are not going to repeat. Use your past experiences to create a more meaningful, rewarding future. Everything that has ever happened in your life—good and bad—has brought you to where you are as you read this sentence. Your experiences have affected your personality, your relationships, your financial situation, and your happiness. Your life is constantly molding you. Every detail is important in one way or another; you just fail to recognize it at the time.

Do you want to settle for a humdrum life? Do you want to look back on a life full of shoulda's, woulda's, and coulda's? If you want a better life, you have to go out and make it happen, no matter what stands in your way. You do not succeed in spite of your obstacles—a rough upbringing, the loss of a job or a loved one, a mental or physical handicap—you succeed because of them. These unexpected experiences can deter you and alter your course. They may slow you down, but they cannot stop you. Rough times teach you a very important life lesson. You are human, and there is nothing wrong with that.

One of my favorite sayings is, "Sometimes you are the windshield. Sometimes you are the bug." Lucky for us our fate is not as bleak. While I have yet to see a bug un-splat itself, we get second chances. If we make a mistake, we get the opportunity to bounce back.

Life is not about the handful of bad things that try to hold you back. It is about the good things that make life worth living. Don't live in fear of what could go wrong. Focus on what could go right. No one in the world can go through life without experiencing failure. Accepting the potential for failure is a necessary fact of life.

My little brother Tanner's dream is to become a professional baseball player. It has been his goal for most of his life, and he has talked about it for years. He is a phenomenal athlete, but if he doesn't make the big leagues, he can still live out his dream to varying degrees. He can get into coaching. He can become a hitting instructor. He can become a talent scout. There are many options. At his disposal is the most precious commodity of all—time. He has enough time to focus 100% on living his dream. The potential for failure should be the last thing on his mind. He has the rest of his life to be ordinary. He can take a shot at an extraordinary life now. Make sure that you take your shot too.

You are the author of your own life. If you are following the advice in this book, you are beginning a new chapter in it. You can choose the setting for your story, but you will have to take some risks. Some people will make small changes like trying a new hobby. Others will make huge changes like taking the leap into a new career field or pursuing a higher education. Some will be starting over completely. The key is to realize that you will not be throwing away your past. You will be using it as a stepping-stone towards your future, learning lessons along the way. I am a great example of this. I completed nine years of schooling to become a chiropractor, and now I am a part-time biology teacher. I never could have imagined the path that my life has taken. Nevertheless, trial and error is an important part of the process of living. You need to forgive yourself and move on. Every mistake can be seen as a learning experience. Ask yourself, "What would I do if I were not afraid?" Then go for it. It is the only way that you will reach your full potential.

> "If you are distressed by anything external, the pain is not due to the thing in itself, but to your estimate of it; and this you have the power to revoke at any moment."
>
> -Marcus Aurelius

Fall in love with yourself

Each of us has something special to offer this world. We have our own natural gifts and talents. God had a very important reason for putting you on this Earth; it is up to you to find out what that reason is. Along the way, you might even fall in love with yourself.

Love is a crucial part of the human experience. Giving and receiving love sustains us and enriches our lives. People that love themselves seem to be satisfied in almost all circumstances, while those who do not can find a way to be unhappy in any situation. If you are hollow and aching inside, nothing you do will bring you the satisfaction that you seek.

People that struggle with their weight are a perfect example. Many overweight people postpone their happiness until the day that they lose the fifty pounds that have been holding them back. The reality is that sometimes that day never comes and they will remain miserable. The only solution is to consciously decide that you are good enough to love yourself now, instead of trying to fit into someone else's idea of beauty.

If you do not love yourself, find out what is missing, and make the necessary changes. Discover how to make you matter to you. Wake up every day saying, "What can I do today to fall deeper in love with me?"

The easiest way to feel good about being you is to focus on the things that you do well and the ways that you make a positive impact on the world. We are all a lot more important than we give ourselves credit for. You need to remind yourself of that every single day.

List at least ten things that you are good at (making people laugh, your job, taking care of your children).

1. I am good at _____
2. I am good at _____
3. I am good at _____
4. I am good at _____
5. I am good at _____
6. I am good at _____
7. I am good at _____
8. I am good at _____
9. I am good at _____
10. I am good at _____

Now list at least ten people, places, or things that you make better just by being alive (your spouse, your home, your pets, your church).

1. I am an asset to _____
2. I am an asset to _____
3. I am an asset to _____
4. I am an asset to _____
5. I am an asset to _____
6. I am an asset to _____
7. I am an asset to _____
8. I am an asset to _____
9. I am an asset to _____
10. I am an asset to _____

These lists will become the foundation of your positive affirmations. These statements are going to remind you that you are a person worthy of love. They will program your brain to use these qualities to attract more passion and joy into your life.

Spend a few minutes reinforcing a positive vision of yourself every day. Try the following strategies to put these affirmations to good use. I have personally used each of them, and they all give me the boost that I need:

- Tape this list onto your bathroom mirror so that it is the first thing that you see when you wake up and the last thing that you see before bed.
- Make a recording of your affirmations. Listen to it every morning on your way to work or while you are preparing for your day.
- Keep a copy of your affirmation in your pocket. Read them whenever you are feeling down or need an emotional boost.
- Give a copy of your affirmations to a loved one. Have them remind you how great you are whenever possible.

Live like a kid again

When we were young, we dreamt about all of the great things that we would accomplish when we grew up. Can somebody tell me why we wanted to do a crazy thing like that? Growing up is completely overrated—kids have it made. They are masters of living in the present. For the most part, childhood is an endless series of positive feelings and happiness. Kids are unconcerned with the future because they are busy experiencing the wonder and excitement of their day-to-day activities.

Time is the great equalizer. Whether you are a bank teller or a movie star, time will catch up with you, no matter how hard you try to fight it. You are going to get old; it doesn't mean that you have to act that way. Wouldn't you like to feel like you did in the happiest days of your childhood? It is less difficult than you might think. Youth is not an age; it is a state of mind. If you can rekindle the feelings of jubilation that you once knew as a child, you can make anything fun—even work. Try these ten examples to get you started:

Childhood:	Youthful Adulthood:
1. Playing in the dirt	Gardening
2. Riding bike	Joining a cycling club
3. Going swimming	Relaxing in the hot tub
4. Playing hide-and-seek	Turning off your cell phone
5. Playing tag	Chasing your spouse around the bedroom
6. Going to the park	Taking a nature hike
7. Jumping off the roof	Sky diving
8. Hiding from the chores	Bringing home take-out
9. Show and tell	Finding pride in your work
10. Going to school	Adult education classes

Wanting to stay young at heart is not just for the immature and the apathetic. Success and a youthful nature can go hand in hand. The author George Mikes is a great example. While researching his book on hypnotherapy, he visited a psychoanalyst. The doctor began by asking Mikes whether he enjoyed a happy childhood. "I," Mikes replied, "am still enjoying a happy childhood."

"It is not easy to find happiness in ourselves, and it is not possible to find it elsewhere."

-American essayist Agnes Repplier

Stay in your comfort zone

They say that to become a success you have to get out of your comfort zone. What is wrong with staying in your comfort zone? Shouldn't comfort be one of the most important things to accomplish in life? We aspire to make our millions so that we can live a life of comfort, but true happiness has been free all along. Find happiness where you are comfortable, don't go looking for it.

One of the biggest problems that I encountered while building my business was that I was constantly pushed out of my comfort zone. I knew that in order to build a thriving clinical practice I had to meet potential patients and give them a reason to come to my clinics. If I wasn't giving health screenings at a shopping center, I was analyzing golf swings at the local country club. I can think of a thousand better ways to spend my time. These uncomfortable tasks made it hard to find joy in my work, and they drained me. I was exhausted—both mentally and physically. It took more energy to get out of my comfort zone than it was worth.

Forget about what society calls success and happiness. Some people have to chase a dream to find happiness. Others find that chasing superficial dreams has caused them to miss out on life. In order for me to be happy, I had to let them go. The only true measure of success is happiness. If you forget to have fun, everything you do becomes a burden.

Forget about what other people think of you. Enjoy your individuality and do not worry about whether or not your desires are comparable to those of your peers. I am now motivated by delight, not approval. You can catch me doing silly things all of the time. If it puts a smile on someone else's face, I have helped make their day a little brighter. If they do not like it, they will just have to get over it. I no longer let other people's opinions of me bring me down. I live my life to maintain my own happiness while trying my best to not cause unhappiness to anyone else. I am finally comfortable in my own skin.

"Time is the coin of your life. It is the only coin you have, and only you can determine how it will be spent. Be careful lest you let other people spend it for you."

-Author Bonnie Friedman

Slowing down in a fast-paced world

Life is a journey, not a destination—stop running so fast. We rush and rush through life, and then we wonder where it has all gone. It would be great if life came with a pause button, but even if it did, we would probably lose the remote in the couch anyhow. We need to find a way to slow down enough to recognize that life is happening right now, at this very moment.

Most people don't even enjoy their leisure time. Either they hurriedly rush through their hobbies or they take them too seriously. Just look at the number of people cursing and throwing things on the golf course. Hobbies are supposed to be relaxing; they are not supposed to increase our stress level. The fix for this problem; if you cannot learn to do something well, learn to enjoy doing it poorly.

Another problem is that our minds never stop running a mile-a-minute. We let our work and our worries invade every second of our waking hours. We even manage to let our problems spill over into our dreams. You need to realize that there is nothing on your to-do list that is worth ruining your life over. Slow is the speed at which we should live.

Try to engage in activities that force you to stay in the moment: singing, spelunking, cycling, performance art. During activities like these, time seems to stand still, and the hyperactivity of your mind subsides. Alternatively, get out into nature. See the majesty of a flowing river, watch a squirrel nibble on an acorn, go bird watching, or just take a walk with your thoughts. While you are enjoying nature, make a mental list of all the things you have been taking for granted. It will help you see what you have been missing.

> "Half our life is spent trying to find something to do with the time we have rushed through life trying to save."
>
> -Actor Will Rogers

Get over yourself

The world survived a long time before you were born, and it will survive long after you are gone. Life is too short to take yourself so seriously. If you do, you will end up seriously unhappy and seriously disappointed.

The key is to put your life into perspective. An unhappy person will complain about a speck of dust in a mansion, while a happy person can make a palace out of a trailer. Embrace the ability to laugh at yourself, to see the bigger picture, and to see that everything will work out. Focus on what you have accomplished, not what you have not. You will be much happier when you realize that you do not have to have an answer for everything. That is what Yahoo and Google are for.

We spend so much time and effort searching for happiness, and often times we realize that we had what we wanted all along. We just needed to get out of our own way. The best example in my life is a small clinic that I owned in Ponca, Nebraska. It took me years of stress and toil to understand how important peace, relaxation, and contentment are to me. I realized that I had already attained these things—before I let them slip through my fingers. I had the opportunity to continue to work at a low stress, low overhead clinic that I loved. I could have spent my free time golfing or relaxing on the river. I could have fallen in love with the pace of life. Nevertheless, I was young and driven, and I could not get out of town fast enough. Oops!

I was constantly craving happiness. That is why I kept changing locations, changing women, and changing vices. I had dozens of girlfriends during this period. It never worked out, but it was rarely their fault. They were not making me happy, but nothing was. I treated life like a competition. If you could bench press two hundred pounds, I would bench press three hundred. If you could see forty patients in a day, I would see sixty. I always wanted to be the best, but it was for a sick need to have people think a certain way about me. It was never really for me, which is why I was never happy. I was living for the approval of others instead of the fulfillment of myself.

Some people go out of their way to take life too seriously. Former Harvard president Charles W. Eliot was one of them. One day Mr. Eliot announced his plans to reduce financial support for the university's baseball team. Pressed for an explanation, Eliot complied, "This year I'm told the team did well because one pitcher had a fine curveball," he declared. "I understand that a curveball is thrown with a deliberate attempt to deceive. Surely that is not an ability we would want to foster at Harvard." The sad thing is that he was able to say this with a straight face.

> "The mark of a successful man is one that has spent an entire day on the bank of a river without feeling guilty about it."
>
> -Author Unknown

Ten ways to take yourself less seriously

1. Sing karaoke. It is impossible to take yourself too seriously while you are butchering the theme song from Grease.
2. Tell jokes. They serve a purpose whether they get a laugh or not.
3. Strike up a conversation with a stranger. You never know the stories that they may have to tell.
4. Talk to yourself. It is only a problem if you start answering yourself.
5. Play in a puddle the next time it rains.
6. Buy a Hula Hoop. Use it often.
7. Get a tattoo. Make it a temporary one if you are afraid of needles.
8. Play with your food. Make a mashed potato volcano. Give your pancakes a bacon smiley face. Eat with your hands.
9. Walk around in your underwear when you are alone in the house.
10. Dance at weddings. Start with the chicken dance. Work up to the robot as your skills improve.

"Slow down and everything you are chasing will come around and catch you."

-Family therapist John De Paola

Life Lessons:

- There are no such things as mistakes—only learning experiences. Don't be afraid to fail every once in a while. Use your past to create a better future. The tough times in your past might be just the motivation that you need.
- Children can teach us a lot about passion and joy. Youth is attainable at any age. Let your inner child out so that you can find true happiness.
- Stop seeking the approval of others. Focus on being the best you possible. Quit worrying about whether or not your desires are comparable to others.
- Stop taking life so seriously. Life is too short to think that you are such a big deal. Live in the moment and enjoy the ride.

Chapter 10

Become a Story Worth Telling: Creating a Passionate Life

"Happiness is the only good. The time to be happy is now. The place to be happy is here. The way to be happy is to make others so."

-Civil war veteran and
orator Robert Green Ingersoll

Life is constantly changing, and each new day brings greater clarity about what is important. The very purpose of life is to evolve and progress toward fulfillment. Giving of yourself is the best way to do this. When you make the lives around you better, your life automatically develops a stronger meaning and sense of purpose.

The best examples that come to my mind are the group of missionaries that I was blessed to meet in 2006. I spearheaded a project to setup a health clinic for seventy missionaries while they were back in the United States between mission trips. The positive energy during the event was exhilarating. Every person that I encountered was living on next to nothing so that they could continue their work, yet they were hungry to find ways to give more of themselves. They were giving their entire lives to a worthy cause, yet they were appreciative of me for the little bit that I did for them. In a world that asks, "What's in it for me?" they ask, "What can I do for you?"

One missionary in particular comes to mind. He is a walking billboard for living a life of purpose. He is not working in a far off land like Africa or Afghanistan. He is ministering to Hollywood. He had been a successful attorney, but something was missing. He wasn't living his purpose. God had bigger plans for his life. He decided to pack up his car and head west. He gave up a life of comfort and privilege to sleep in his car; trusting God to provide for his future. He has not completely transformed Hollywood yet, but he is making a difference in peoples' lives every day. Moreover, he has never been more excited to get up in the morning.

On the flipside, many successful people are aching on the inside. They look like they have a full life, but they feel empty. They have all of the money that they can spend, but they are missing something. They have a life with value, but not values. They cannot reach their full potential for happiness because they haven't found the purpose or meaning for their life. They have yet to feel the pride and satisfaction that comes with making this world a better place.

You do not have to take a vow of poverty and move to a foreign country to find a sense of purpose. Different people find meaning in different things. You may find your calling by volunteering at a homeless shelter, raising your children, working for a value-based company, or coaching young athletes. The important thing is to choose your purpose in accordance with your own values rather than conforming to others' expectations. It makes no difference what your life looks like from the outside; it is what it looks like to you that matters most. Those who work at something that they love—business, philanthropy, the healing arts, or charity—can sleep better at night and feel good about their contribution to the world.

> "Try not to become a man of success but rather to become a man of value."
>
> -Albert Einstein

The purpose of life is a life of purpose

Live a life worth living. Become a story worth telling. Be a person worth remembering.

Writing these words immediately makes me think about a man who had a major impact on my life—Jerry O'Neill. My uncle Jerry had a fun-loving way about him that allowed him to be happy and at peace in any situation. His long battle with cancer taught him to live every day as if it was his last. It made him see the world through wider, wiser eyes. He never complained, and he lived his life more fully than any healthy person I have ever known. He didn't let chronic pain keep him from being a great father. He didn't let chemotherapy keep him from his work and his social life. He didn't let his obvious mortality steal his smile. He made every second count. His soul remained full of life, even while his body failed him. He refused to be beaten. Unfortunately, it took his death for me to fully appreciate the gifts that he had been giving me all along.

Jerry O'Neill is a story worth telling. Every person that knew him has a favorite memory to share. They may not all be G-rated, but they are great stories nonetheless. They are chapters in the life of a man who played the cards he was dealt and thoroughly enjoyed the ride. He has left his fingerprints on thousands of people and millions of memories. His life embodied the saying, "You can count the number of seeds in an apple, but you cannot count the number of apples in a seed." He is always with me—his memory, his spirit, his energy. I take him with me. His memory and impact will never die.

Jerry's death helped me to see the absurdity of the pace at which we live this precious life. He was an incredible teacher and I learned so much from him. Not necessarily from the words he spoke, but from the way he acted—especially when he was at his sickest. He taught me to be more conscious of the power of the moment. He taught me that I do not want to be known as a doctor or a teacher—I want to be known as someone that has influenced people in a positive way. I want my future children to be able to look up to me. I want my parents to be proud of the man that I have become. I thank him for that, and I hope that these words will inspire you to do more with your life as well.

Find your passion and awe

> "If you observe a really happy man you will find him building a boat, writing a symphony, educating his son, growing double dahlias in his garden, or looking for dinosaur eggs in the Gobi desert. He will not be searching for happiness as if it were a collar button that has rolled under the radiator. He will not be striving for it as a goal in itself. He will have become aware that he is happy in the course of living life twenty-four crowded hours in a day."
>
> -Australian psychiatrist W. Beran Wolfe

Everyone could use more passion in their life. I hope that you find it in your family. If not, you need to find it in some other facet of your life. Find something that makes you happy and increases the optimism that you feel about the future. I found that passion in the game of baseball.

I love baseball because it represents more than a game to me. It represents beautiful August days, families spending time together, and the appreciation that comes with watching a man throw his heart and soul into something that he loves. My love for baseball is best summed up by the words of the former New York Yankee Jim Bouton, when he said, "A ballplayer spends a good piece of his life gripping a baseball, and in the end, it turns out that it was the other way around all the time." The moral; the hobbies and activities that we take part in will always give us more than we can give back. I could write 30 books that sell 10,000,000 copies, and my writing would never have a larger affect on the world than it has on me while I write it.

I see many similarities between the game of life and the game of baseball:
- They are both meant to be fun.

- Neither is meant to be taken too seriously. You have to be able to relax or you will never succeed.
- No one is perfect. If you get 3 hits out of every 10 at-bats, you are one of the best players in the world.
- It is a game that needs individual excellence, but it is impossible to win without the help of others.
- You have to be in the moment. The season is 162 games long. That is 1458 innings, but the only pitch that matters is the next one.

The opposite of passion is boredom. I will be the first to admit that I used to be a bore. I read the Almanac for fun—in case I ever made it on Jeopardy—and I had a turkey sandwich on toast with no mayo or cheese every day for two years. Boredom makes it hard to get out of bed and it saps your energy and motivation. I was stuck in a rut disguised as responsibility. Do not let it happen to you.

If you are true to your passions, your life will shine. If you deny them, your life will suck. In the end, the power lies in your hands. It is an amazing thing to see someone that has found something that makes him or her feel truly alive. When you are true to your passions, you feel more alive at the end of the day than when it began. Choose whether you want to live a boring life, or an inspired life of passion. Have an answer when someone asks, "What will the best and most amazing experience of your life look like?"

> "Dying is no big deal, living is the trick."
>
> -Sportswriter Red Smith

Seven more steps to a passionate life

In a perfect world, all of the information in this book would be a quick and easy recipe for an enchanted life. Changing your life is going to take time. However, there are some quick fixes that you can use to quickly improve your life while you are working on your long-term goals.

"What lies behind us and what lies before us are small matters compared to what lies within us."

-Author Ralph Waldo Emerson

1. Accept what you have

The problem with many people is that they always think that they will be happy when they reach a certain destination—a new job, retirement, or winning the lottery. Unfortunately, it takes time to get there, and by the time you arrive, you might have a new destination in mind. Instead, try being happy with where you are, with who you are, and with what you have.

I used to take pride in the things that I owned and the money in my wallet. Now I take pride in the relationships that I have. I used to be jealous of people who had more than I did, but now I am happy for them.

Action Steps: Don't compare what you have with those who have more than you do. Compare yourself with those who have less, with those who are going through tragedy, and with those who are struggling. You will see that you are extremely blessed.

2. Enjoy the simple pleasures

You can find these everywhere: A beautiful sunset, the smell of fresh-cut grass, a giggling baby, a good book, and dancing in the rain. These things break up the monotony of the day and make the journey more enjoyable.

Action Steps: Make a list of twenty simple pleasures in your life—things you enjoy that you could find every day. I will get you started with some of my own:

1. Hot towels fresh out of the dryer.
2. Laughing so hard it hurts.
3. Getting good mail.
4. Waking up and realizing you still have a few more hours to sleep.
5. Hearing your favorite song on the radio.
6. Finding twenty dollars in your coat from last winter.
7. Holding hands with someone that you love.

Make time for these simple pleasures throughout the day. Do something good for yourself every chance that you get.

3. Limit your information intake

We are assaulted with information every waking moment: E-mail, Web sites, newspapers, magazines, television, radio, and cell phones. Technology is moving faster than our brains can manage. We do too much in a short amount of time without the ability to experience any of it. Not only can technology distract you, it can overwhelm you. Technological overload fills up your life until you have no time for more important things.

Action Steps: Determine what you can live without. Remember that the cell phone was originally designed for emergencies, not to allow you to be reached every second of every day. Limit the use of text messaging and e-mailing; it is extremely impersonal. It also takes all of the passion out of a conversation. If you want to speak with someone, call them or stop in for a visit. Do not think about what you are giving up; focus on what you are gaining: time, freedom, and happiness.

4. Single-task

I do not believe in multitasking. Instead, focus on one task at a time. This leads to increased productivity and decreased stress. Trying to do too many things at one time is counterproductive. Doing two things at once results in neither being done wholly.

Action Steps: Tackle one thing at a time. If you are interrupted while you are in the middle of something, decide which needs to be handled now, and handle it.

5. Go outdoors

Humans are highly civilized and evolved animals. But, biologically speaking, we are animal's nonetheless. Our maker wants us to enjoy the wonderful world that He has created for us. Unfortunately, many of us spend all of our time indoors. If we are not at work, we are in the car, or on the couch.

Action Steps: Get outdoors so that you can appreciate nature, the beauty of the world around us, and the fun of physical activity. The sunlight will be good for your complexion, and the fresh air will do wonders for your spirit.

"There is nothing like returning to a place that remains unchanged to find the ways in which you yourself have altered."

-Nelson Mandela

6. Associate with happy people

Some people are born to hip-hop through life; others are born to sing the blues. You need to spend time with the former while avoiding the latter. It is an amazing thing to be in the presence of someone that is truly happy. If you are around people who are happier than you are their emotional state will be infectious. Learn from them.

Action Steps: Do not envy people who are happy. On the contrary, be happy for them and spend time near them.

7. Wake up earlier than you have to

There is nothing worse than starting your day behind the eight ball. You are in a cranky mood, you have to rush through your morning routine, and there is no time to plan and prepare for your day. Why not give yourself an extra thirty minutes in the morning so that you are not stressed and depressed before you ever walk out your front door.

I have found this to be an amazing change in my life. It has made the start of my days more positive, and I now have time to read the sports page, exercise, and enjoy a breakfast that does not pop out of the toaster.

Action Steps: Start by waking up thirty minutes earlier than usual. Do something that makes you a better person.

Life Lessons:

- The only truth about life is that it is going to change. Go with the flow and be open to this change. Your life purpose will make itself evident if you keep your eyes and ears peeled. Jump at the chance to give of yourself and make the lives around you better.
- Many people are successful in their career while lacking in the rest of their life. They have an empty feeling that comes from living a self-centered life. You cannot find complete happiness if your life doesn't have a deeper meaning. You will not be at peace until you find a way to leave the world a better place than you found it.
- Find that thing that makes you feel truly alive. Fill your life with so much passion that you cannot wait to get up in the morning. Share that joyful feeling with others.

Chapter 11

Never Stop Learning: Ignite Your Spark

"To see a world in a grain of sand, and heaven in a wild flower, hold infinity in the palm of your hand, and eternity in an hour."

-English poet William Blake

The most difficult conversation that I have ever had was when I told my father that I was selling my clinics and starting my life over. I confided in him that I felt hurt and disappointed by how things had unfolded. I was stunned that a quality education, a Midwestern work ethic, and a big smile were not enough. Being the best and the brightest did not matter as much in the real world as it had in school. I was frustrated, and I wanted answers.

My new career path as a biology professor has put me in a special position to reevaluate the educational system. I am able to view the situation from a unique position. I love being a teacher, but I am young enough to remember what it is like to be a student trying to get by. Several important truths have come from this. Things that my high school guidance counselor failed to mention. Things that the educational community may not want you to know. My chief concern is that we may have been misled all along.

Let down by the promise of an education

One evening, at a dinner held in his honor, Harvard president Charles W. Eliot was regaled by toasts from several professors. "Since you became president," one colleague enthused, "Harvard has become a storehouse of knowledge."

"What you say is true, but I can claim little credit for it," Eliot replied. "It is simply that the freshmen bring so much in, and the seniors take so little away!"

An education does not necessarily prepare you to succeed in the real world. Our educational system is heavily weighted towards information, and sorely lacking in inspiration. School—for the most part—does not teach students how to think, only how to please instructors. Not how to create, only to inform.

I thank my Talented and Gifted (TAG) program instructors in high school for teaching me the real meaning of an education. We focused on brainstorming, creative thinking, and problem solving exercises. They showed me that the importance of an education was not in the subject matter, but in learning how to value knowledge and think for myself. It prepared me for a true liberal arts education after high school, and it was very freeing.

I went on to college, full of hope and expectations. I was taking up to thirty credit hours a semester, so my education consumed my life. I knew that it would be hard work, but that was not a new thing for me. I understood the importance of an education, and I was fixated on the future.

Going through school, I knew that I was going to be a great doctor. I was the youngest person to ever graduate from Northwestern Health Sciences University. I saw more patients than any intern in university history. I was receiving referrals from licensed doctors sixteen months before I graduated. I was well on my way toward a career worth envying. My teachers—and my grades—all but guaranteed my success.

The respect and admiration pushed me. I went to dozens of business building seminars. I devoured information about how to manage a successful clinical practice. I filled journal after journal with "million dollar" ideas. My business plans and marketing ideas were flawless. Several of my classmates placed bets on how long it would take me to make my first million dollars. If anyone had earned the right to be a success, it was I.

I left the safe confines of school with a back full of pats and a false sense of security. I had prepared my entire life for graduation, and I assumed that a successful career was handed to you on the way out the door. I thought that I was ready for life after school, but it only took a couple of months to realize that I had been duped. My professors never said it would be so darn hard.

I think that part of the problem is that teachers only tell half of the story. They tend to sugarcoat things, shielding students from how difficult the real world can be. For instance, my high school accounting teacher had me believing that all accountants earn six-figure salaries at Fortune 500 companies. He neglected to give equal time to the bookkeepers that work the overnight shift at the Motel 6 by the highway rest stop.

I enjoy teaching nursing and pre-med students, and occasionally I am blessed with a student that thirsts for a knowledge of the human body. Student's that are passionate about learning are the reason that I get out of bed in the morning. As a teacher, I want my students to be optimistic about the future, but my turbulent life has made me believe in incorporating a healthy dose of cautious realism. My students are looking for a better life, and I *want* them to graduate excited, but I *need* them to graduate prepared.

I am not trying to blame teachers either. While some have control over their curriculum, most are on a short leash. Teachers have to play the game as well. Their job is to give students the information that they need to move on to the next academic level. They have to prepare students for their basic skills tests and their SAT's. If an educator gets too liberal with his or her methods, they become the tall blade of grass that is the first to be cut. They have to play by the rules in order to maintain their job security—and their schools accreditation.

As far as school administrators are concerned, a teacher's job is to teach; a student's job is to learn. To them, academia is a black and white world of absolutes. However, the real world is full of nuances and shades of gray. It is easy to see why I feel caught in the middle. The teacher in me says that it is the students' responsibility to gain worldly experience on their own time, while the student in me thinks that it is the schools responsibility to prepare them for life after graduation.

The entire educational system is flawed because it does not foster greatness. If a student spends their time learning things that they are passionate about, they may not pass their required courses. They feel like they are forced to cram enough information to make it through the next test. On the flipside, if a teacher spends too much time "reaching" their students, they get behind in their lesson plans and their students suffer on their standardized tests.

I know that many people think that I am a cynic, but I do not feel that way. A cynic is someone that is prone to doubt. I am the polar opposite. There is no doubt in my mind that our schools have the potential for greatness. I may have some negative viewpoints, but I am full of hope. While our educational system may not be perfect, I still love it for what it has the potential to become. Perfect or not, you need to understand the important role that knowledge plays in discovering the best life possible.

The benefits of an education

One day an organ grinder, stationed outside Pietro Mascagni's apartment, began playing tunes from his opera—Cavalleria Rusticana—at roughly half the proper speed. Irritated, the composer rushed into the street.

"I am Mascagni," he told the organ grinder. "Let me show you how to play this music correctly." With that, he gave the organ's handle several energetic turns and retired to his room.

The next day Mascagni was irked to hear the infernal organ grinder outside his window once again, still playing at an absurdly slow pace. However, the man had made one significant change to his routine. Peeking out his window, Mascagni was dismayed to find, posted above the man's head, a newly erected sign reading: "PUPIL OF MASCAGNI." Much to Mascagni's chagrin, the organ grinder's business flourished. I guess what they say is true; a bad education is better than no education at all.

Everyone has a unique reason for pursuing an education. Whatever your reason, make sure that you are passionate about your chosen field of study. Of the many benefits of an education, the most important benefit is…the education. Knowledge is the key to a passionate life, and the war against ignorance must be fought every day. You can never go wrong if you finish every day a little smarter than you started it. Here are a few questions to get you thinking, no pun intended.

1. What type of classes would you be interested in taking for fun (psychology, genetics, world religions)?

_____

_____

_____

2. Are there everyday topics that you would like to know more about (computers, engines, food, global warming)?

_____

_____

3. What events in our history would you like to explore (WWII, Vietnam, religious history)?

_____

_____

_____

The most powerful question in the English language is, "Why?" I love to know how things work, including bodily functions. My multiple degrees and career choices have all come from my need to understand the many intricacies of the human body. I hope that you can find something that you are as excited about as I have. It will take you places that you have only dreamt about. You will find the right path for your life, which in turn may lead you to happiness and financial reward.

Researcher Sally Blotnick interviewed 1500 recent graduates about their career plans—and the basis for their decisions. 83% were motivated by money and wanted to make as much as possible as soon as possible. 17% were determined to follow their passion. Twenty years later, 101 of them had become millionaires. 100 of these millionaires were from the 17% who followed their passions.[28]

While education does not guarantee success, studies have consistently shown that the more educated you are, the higher your tax bracket. In 2005, the Bureau of Labor and Statistics studied how income correlates with different degrees.[29] Here are their findings:

Median weekly earnings for different education levels:	
High School graduate	$583/wk
Associate degrees	$699/wk
Bachelor's degree	$937/wk
Master's degree	$1129/wk
Doctoral degree	$1421/wk

Millionaire or not, there are huge financial incentives for obtaining an education. However, the effect that an education will have on your time and your happiness are more important.

Many professions have an inverse relationship between education level and the amount of arduous work that will be asked of them. Compare the job description of a Certified Nursing Assistant (CNA) to that of a Registered Nurse (RN). Or a mid-level associate at a law firm relative to one of the partners.

People without an education are often times forced to do the dirty work. In my own clinical practices, every five minutes that I spent with my patients made at least twenty minutes of work for my support staff. While I was treating patients or working at my mahogany desk, my employees were busy doing the laundry, handling telemarketing calls, and fighting with unrelenting insurance companies.

An education can oftentimes help you discover ways to build a better work-life balance. The more specialized your skills, the more concessions your employer will make to keep you happy. Perhaps you will be able to create a flexible schedule, or work from home. The right education will make your options endless. You owe it to yourself to take your best shot.

The final benefit of an education is the options that it affords you. There are an increasing number of creative ways that you can use an education. Perhaps it could be consulting work, working for an online company, or teaching. The only thing that can limit your options is your own mind.

I am living proof of this. I was able to make changes in my life quite easily because I was able to use my education in an alternative manner. 100% of my income now comes from work that involves using my education in a different way. I have used my knowledge of the human body—and my biology education—to become a biology professor. I have also transformed my education into a lucrative consulting and speaking career. I have found a way to use my education to earn a living without treating a single patient.

> "I could have been a doctor, but there were too many good shows on TV."
>
> -Australian humorist Jason Love

You do not always need a traditional education

When she was twenty-six years old, Jane Goodall went to Africa, where she met legendary archaeologist and anthropologist Louis Leakey. Though Goodall was concerned about her lack of education, Leakey enlisted her to serve as his personal assistant. In fact, Leakey had hired her precisely because her mind had not been muddled with academic notions. He was able to teach her how things work in the jungle instead of the classroom.

Bill Gates and Michael Dell both dropped out of college. Peter Jennings and Chris Rock got their GED's. Henry Ford, Andrew Carnegie, Thomas Edison, and Mark Twain never even graduated high school. These examples prove that a traditional education is not always necessary to succeed. More importantly, it shows that the key to success is passion and determination.

I am not saying that an education is not important. It is the exact opposite. These people are exceptions, not the rule. I think that a traditional education is a major factor in success. However, I believe that there is a different kind of education that can prepare you as well—a real-world education.

I was first told that I was a genius when I was nine, but genius is only as good as the task that you are trying to accomplish. I will admit that I have been blessed in several areas, but I have seen real-world geniuses that can interact with children or the handicapped in a way that blows my mind. Everyone is an expert at something; the key is to find out what that something is. You do not need a formal education to be a bright and creative person. You just need to excel in the classroom of life.

> "One definition of success is having more time to spend on the things that you value outside of work. The goal should be to have a lot of free time to be."
>
> -author unknown

The education paradox

Thanks to community colleges and online educational programs, it is never too late to go back to school. It will take time and money to get an education, but it will pay dividends forever. This is what I call the education paradox. You will have to make sacrifices that will create some difficulty in the present, but you will gain an entirely new future.

Community colleges offer the flexibility needed to balance school with family, work, and other priorities. Over 80% of community college students work at least part-time, and the average age of a community college student is twenty-nine.[30] Millions of people are going back to school to create a brighter tomorrow, and they are better late than never.

This is part of the reason that community colleges are becoming an increasingly important part of the American educational system. According to the American Association of Community Colleges, there are currently 11.5 million students enrolled at a community college[31], and many of them are vying for a second shot at life. They know that the shortest distance between where they are and where they want to be is a better education.

Life Lessons:

- Being the best and the brightest in school does not guarantee success in the real world. The entire educational system is flawed because it does not foster greatness. It only teaches students how to jump through hoops. Maybe someone should have warned us that life after school would be such a bumpy ride.

- Everyone has his or her own educational goals and needs. Whatever your reason, make sure that you are passionate about your pursuits. Knowledge is the key to success, and an education allows you to create your own luck. The more that you know, the more that you can become.

- A real-world education is as important as any other kind. Everyone is a genius in his or her own right. The key is to find an area where you excel. Creativity and knowledge are not exclusive to the classroom. The classroom of life is just as important.

Part III: Love Your Livelihood

"In order that people may be happy at work, these three things are needed: They must be fit for it. They must not do too much of it. And they must have a sense of success in it."

-Social critic John Ruskin

Chapter 12

No One Wins the Rat Race: Working in a Burned-Out World

"The problem with the rat race is that even if you win, you're still a rat."

-Comedian Lily Tomlin

"What has become of my life?"

How many times have you muttered this under your breath while you grind through another day at the office?

We work more hours than our parents did. We take less vacation time than ever before. Our family life suffers because we have more work to do in less time. Work puts us on a treadmill that we cannot keep up with—running a race that nobody wins. We have finally reached our breaking point.

Despite our best efforts to manage our time—and the many devices designed to make life easier—our lives are filled to the brim. Modern conveniences like computers, fax machines, cell phones, and the internet create more stress than they relieve. Instead of accomplishing the same amount of work in less time, we are given more work, and pushed to do it faster. One person is now forced to do the work of two or three in an era of downsizing, cost cutting, international competition, and advanced technology. This increased demand on our time has left us feeling insecure, stressed, and overwhelmed.

Where do these problems with work-life balance and job satisfaction come from? What has changed in our world that has allowed this to happen? More importantly, how can we stop it before it is too late?

Understanding job satisfaction

The nature of job satisfaction has been studied and discussed since the early 1920's. It is complicated due to its subjective nature. The disappointing truth is that understanding job satisfaction—or the lack thereof—seems to be more important than bringing about enough change to make it a reality.

My initial research led me to the job satisfaction studies of Andrew Oswald—a Professor of Economics at the University of Warwick. His research has consistently shown that job satisfaction has been on the decline among workers of all ages and income brackets since the early 1970's.[32] Whether you are a thirty-five year old man bringing in thirty thousand dollars a year, or a fifty-four year old woman commanding a six-figure income, you are probably less happy with your work now than you were five years ago. Moreover, this problem will continue to get worse until you decide to do something about it.

What makes us unhappy at work?

A reporter once asked the infamous Willie Sutton why he robbed banks. His response: "because that's where the money is." The same can be said about work. Many of us engage in work that doesn't excite us or make us happy. We simply show up day after day because that is where the paycheck is.

A 2003 survey of over 36,000 internet users found that 83% of people are not happy with their jobs.[33] I wanted to find out why, so I surveyed five hundred people that have been employed for at least two years. I asked them what makes them unhappy with their work. The top eight responses that I received will not surprise you. However, which ones made the top of the list might.

Top eight causes of unhappiness at work

1. I work too many hours
2. I dislike my boss
3. I have a rigid schedule; I am unable to take time off for personal or family reasons
4. I have an uncompetitive salary and/or benefits package
5. I receive no recognition for going the extra mile
6. I dislike dealing with customers/unhappy people
7. My employer doesn't care about me as an individual
8. I have no opportunity for advancement

It is very telling that money and advancement are not as important as most people assume. At one time, the only thing that mattered was finding a job that paid the bills and kept food on the table. Now we are awakening to the truth that time and happiness are more precious than money.

Unstable work in an unstable world

A story about the showman P.T. Barnum sheds interesting light on the nature of today's workforce. Early in his career, Barnum created an exhibit, entitled "The Happy Family," consisting of a cage housing a lion, a tiger, a panther—and a baby lamb. The remarkable display earned Barnum unprecedented publicity and attendance figures. Sometime after its opening, Barnum was asked about his plans for the happy family. "The display will become a permanent feature," he declared, "if the supply of lambs holds out."

Work is intrinsically insecure in today's climate. Being a useful employee does not mean that you are irreplaceable. Gone are the "golden watch" days when employers felt like they owed job security to their employees. Many of today's employees will have to move from job to job ten times or more. Many others will tolerate a disappointing job for years—even decades. Financial burdens keep them from leaving their job to find work that would bring them joy.

They know that rocking the boat will make dangerous waves, so they fall in line. They never take the time to explore who they are and what type of work fits them.

A recent Gallup poll found that 55% of employees have no enthusiasm for their work. Another 54% said that they are not utilizing their skills in their current job.[34,35] Laziness and the safety of a steady paycheck cause them to stay put. Cautious people are just happy to have a job to begin with. It is inconvenient and scary to have to start over. They put off any shot at happiness until someday; that mythical time that never seems to arrive.

There are two dynamics at war within you: the desire to be happy and the desire for security. It is common to get excited about change, and then we start to worry about the negatives. We talk ourselves out of great opportunities under the guise of responsibility. Things like family issues or money trouble get us off track. The difficulty is that once a train is derailed, it is nearly impossible to get it back on the track.

There is no such thing as job security any more. According to the Bureau of Labor and Statistics, 3.6 million workers were displaced from jobs that they had held for at least three years between 2005 and 2007. The number of jobless Americans hit an annual average of 8.77 million in 2003, a steep climb from a little over 5.1 million in 2000.[36] With so many companies cleaning house, workers are reexamining their self-worth and facing the fact that they are disposable. Many people are trying to prepare themselves for the fact that they may be looking for work. This time they want to get it right.

Work fast, look scared

One of my brothers works in a very high-pressure industry. The hours are long, the work is hard, and his boss is wound as tight as a spring. Uncertainty reigns as people walk the halls silently, head down, trying to appear pensive, focused, and busy—hoping to avoid being next in line for layoffs or pay cuts. The lesson his coworkers taught him on day one: "Work fast, look scared." This kind of pressure can turn a lump of coal into a diamond, and a good employee into a basket case.

Society rewards success and favors the aggressive. We give too much to careers that do not return the favor. We work at a pace that we cannot keep in order to get ahead in life. All this, coupled with longer hours and handling the workload of two people, can easily lead to trouble.

I began to learn this difficult lesson early on in life. I started working at six in the morning on my sixteenth birthday, and I have never stopped. I worked thirty-five hours a week through high school and college. I constantly gave 100% because it was what my boss and my parents expected of me. It was the only way that I knew how to work.

The attitude I had towards my work was how I dealt with every part of my life. Anything worth doing was worth doing well. I knew that my diligence would pay off someday. Postponing happiness to become a success seemed like a small price to pay. After all, I was already miles ahead of my classmates. By the time I graduated high school, I had completed two years worth of college coursework and I was investing in annuities.

Nine years of school, seven clinics, and three thousand patients later, I still felt the same way. I was a success, but there was no way that I could keep up the pace. I felt like I was destined for greatness, but I was out of energy. I had burned the candle at both ends for so long that I was burnt to a crisp.

I loved my work, but I had reached my breaking point. I was in perpetual motion, constantly craving rest. I was brain dead, and I had to get away. Colleagues and patients begged me to stay, but I resisted because I could no longer find that sense of satisfaction. I was spent.

Do you feel as "used up" as I did? If so, you may be suffering from a condition I call Jobus Overworkus, more commonly known as burnout. Burnout is a state of emotional and physical exhaustion caused by excessive, prolonged stress. It can happen whenever you feel overwhelmed—unable to meet constant demands. Burnout can weaken your immune system, and it has been linked to migraines, digestive disorders, high blood pressure, and heart disease.

People who suffer from burnout describe a sensation of emptiness. A major sign of burnout is the feeling that your efforts are worthless. You have reached the point where the increasing work demands simply become too much. The ability to perform your work is intact, but the spirit to perform it is gone.

No one is immune from burnout. Any person in any profession is susceptible. However, some job types lead to burnout more often than others do. Caregivers, service providers, people with demanding time schedules, and people that perform repetitive, detailed work have the highest risk of burning out.

Many people in the business world live by a survival of the fittest code. In some professions, burnout is considered a status symbol. This is especially true in the helping professions. According to the New York Bar Association, turnover rates among mid-level associates in New York City law firms are 36% every year.[37] At the same time, The United Federation of Teachers found that 45% of New York City public school teachers quit by year five.[38] The unlucky casualties that are lost to burnout are considered an acceptable cost of doing business. The ones that survive wear it like a badge of honor. Nevertheless, burnout should never be seen as a noble affliction. Ruining your life to get ahead is not part of God's plan.

"One of the symptoms of an approaching nervous breakdown is the belief that one's work is terribly important."

-British historian Bertrand Russell

Symptoms of Jobus Overworkus

According to the Maslach Burnout Inventory, there are six issues that can lead to burnout[39]: working too much, working in an unjust environment, working with little social support, working with little or no control, working in a company with poor values, and working for insufficient reward (money, prestige, positive feedback). If this sounds like your work life, be on the lookout for the signs of burnout.

If you are able to recognize them, you can take steps to stop it before it consumes you. Some of the symptoms of burnout include:

- Emotional exhaustion
- Cynicism
- Hopelessness
- Despair
- Frustration
- Irritability
- Detachment
- Isolation

Ignoring these signs is like ignoring a toothache. The pain from your tooth is a warning that something is wrong. Ignoring it, or killing the pain—with drugs or alcohol—does not make the decay or infection go away. In fact, it will only get worse.

Burnout victims have learned that they cannot control their respective worlds, so they stop trying. Their problems seem insurmountable, everything looks bleak, and they cannot muster up the energy to care.

Some specific red flags serve as a warning that your work has pushed you to the limit. You have reached your breaking point when you:

1. Develop a short fuse towards your friends, family, and co-workers
2. Stare at the clock until it strikes 5:00
3. Start to find reasons to call in "sick"
4. Start to forget about the good things you used to enjoy about your work
5. Want nothing to do with your co-workers outside of work
6. Become increasingly upset when you are asked to work late or come in on your day off
7. Develop physical symptoms—nausea, heartburn, headaches, back pain—especially on Monday morning

Burnout is characterized by disengagement and depression. You are merely going through the motions and drawing a paycheck. If all you are receiving from your work is money, you are being grossly underpaid. Either you need to make some serious changes, or you need to consider finding a new line of work.

Cool the burnout sensation

Harold Alexander, the former governor general of Canada, had a curious way of dealing with unfinished business. At the end of the day, he would empty his "In" tray…into his "Out" tray, sending many unopened letters on their way. Alexander was once asked about this peculiar habit. "It saves time," he explained. "You'd be surprised how little of it comes back!"

While you may not be in a position of power that allows this method, it proves an important point. Many of the things that weigh us down at work are not as important as we make them out to be. While everything in this book will help you lead a life that is less susceptible to burnout, there are some specific steps that will ensure your success.

The six-step burnout antidote:

1. Find a new job, or a different career path

According to a recent Integra Realty survey, only one in five people have found what they consider to be the right work for themselves.[40] Sometimes the best solution is to bust out of your rut and get out while your sanity is intact. Too often, however, burnout victims quit an unsatisfactory job without analyzing the source of their dissatisfaction. Oftentimes their next job is as bad as the last one, if not worse. Make sure that you understand what makes you unhappy about your current job so that you can keep from repeating the same mistakes.

Find a job that does not upset your life. Be picky, but not too picky. There is not a job in the world that can satisfy you all of the time. The best that you can hope for is more great days than good and more good days than bad.

2. Modify your current job

If you cannot get out of your current job, you need to alter how you think about it. Most jobs have some built in leeway to tailor them to your unique work style. The ability to mesh your job to your values increases your feelings of control and the enjoyment of your work. Take advantage of your jobs ambiguity and shape it according to your skills and interests.

Review all of your work activities. There must be some parts of your job that you enjoy more than others. Expand the parts of your job that you love. When you see a problem, consider how you can convert it into an opportunity. Let your job evolve around you.

3. Give yourself a break

While burnout is not a purely American disease, it does expose our insane work culture. The Families and Work Institute found that nearly one-third of American workers feel overwhelmed by their job.[41] While we are busy working ourselves to death, European employees are extremely productive while working 35-hour work weeks and taking 8 weeks of vacation per year.[42]

Carrying the weight of the world is hard. Just ask Atlas. If you think that you have to do everything by yourself, you are saying that you don't trust anyone else to help you. Successful people are good at delegating. If you resist delegation, you end up doing all kinds of things that you do not want or need to do. No wonder you feel overwhelmed and your job is pushing you to the limit.

We are conditioned to be competitive instead of supportive. Learn to relax and go with the flow. Reduce your commitments at work, and say no when you have to. Your productivity will soar, and your emotional health will be spared.

4. Quit following the herd

Playing by the rules and towing the company line makes your boss happy, not you. Maintain a balance between going where you want to go, and being happy as you get there.

Hold yourself accountable. Reward yourself, manage your productivity, and monitor your progress. Remember the principle of inertia. An object in motion tends to stay in motion. Use small steps to keep yourself moving toward your goals.

5. Develop a support system

A strong support system, made up of family, friends, and co-workers, can help buffer you against the negative effects of stress and burnout.

Many of us—especially men—are taught that asking for help is a sign of weakness. We all need help from time to time. Accepting support is a sign of maturity and strength. When you allow others to assist you, you bestow a great gift on them. You let them show you how much they care about you.

6. Take better care of yourself

Burnout is a mismatch between effort and recovery. Proper relaxation allows your body to rest, repair, and prepare for optimal function. Your leisure time must restore you, or it is not helping.

Manage your stress. Manage your time. Get plenty of rest. Eat a healthy diet.

Take your full lunch break every day. Listen to music. Exercise. Maintain a sense of humor.

Life Lessons:

- We cannot keep the pace that we have set for our lives. Our work has pushed us to the edge. We are taken prisoner by schedules, job descriptions, and deadlines. If you cannot find happiness at work, the rest of your life will suffer.
- Job satisfaction has been on the decline for an entire generation. There is no end in sight to this problem until we realize that there has to be a better way to live.
- Your employer doesn't feel like they owe you anything. In the current work climate, they believe that you should feel lucky to have a job. Many of them pile on more abuse than you deserve. They are relying on the fact that you are too scared to leave for work that would bring you joy.
- Do not let burnout eat at you. Burnout is brought on by excessive and prolonged stress. It can happen whenever you feel overwhelmed by the constant demands of the daily grind. Nevertheless, there is hope. There are many things that you can do to tap on the brakes and depressurize.

Chapter 13

A Price Too Steep: The Truth about Success

> "Before we set our hearts too much upon anything, let us examine how happy they are, who already possess it."
>
> -French classical author Francois Duc de La Rochefoucauld

Many people are of the opinion that money and success is a clear path to an enchanted life. Hardworking members of the lower and middle class are led to believe that their bosses spend their weekends sipping Long Island iced teas at the country club. This assumption has contributed to much of the increasing tension in the workplace, and it is simply not true.

In a quality of life study of ten thousand managers, Professor Gary Cooper found that 30-40% of manager's work more than 51 hours a week and 66% of supervisors work most of the weekend.[43] Two out of three executives say that their job is hurting their relationships with their spouse and their children.[44] It is clear that "successful" people may not be that successful after all. Many of them have lost their way on their own search for happiness. They are losing the game of life because they do not know the rules.

Doctors and lawyers make great examples. They make a lot of money, but many of them are unhappy. Healthcare and law are high-pressure, cutthroat businesses that demand a lot from their professionals. My clinical practice was controlled by insurance company denials, HIPPA compliance reviews, and escalating patient co-pays. Patients on a tight budget had to decide whether to pay me fifty dollars or take thirty cents worth of aspirin. It is no wonder that the risks for depression, alcoholism, drug abuse, and suicide are alarmingly high in these professions.

Researchers from John Hopkins University found that lawyers suffer Major Depressive Disorder (MDD) at a rate 360% higher than non-lawyers do.[45] At the same time, physicians have the highest suicide rate of any profession[46] All of this points to the fact that many doctors and lawyers are as unhealthy as they are unhappy. Nevertheless, everyone wants to be them because of the money, the prestige, the titles, and the respect.

One explanation for these problems is that there is a large emotional toll that comes with helping others. Doctors, lawyers, nurses, ministers, and social workers spend so much time dealing with the concerns of others that they forget to worry about themselves. They convince themselves that the long hours and the stress are worth the satisfaction that comes with making the world a better place. Problems arise when these caregivers have to constantly sacrifice their personal life for the sake of their professional life. They deny their own happiness in exchange for the happiness of others. The battle for their time, energy, and emotions begins before the ink has had time to dry on their diplomas.

I found this out after a couple of months in clinical practice. I worked all day, and then I brought work home to finish in front of the television. There were many mornings that I was too busy to go to the gym, and there were many evenings that I was too exhausted to spend time with my loved ones.

While the hours were tiring, the emotional toll that my practice took on me was the most exhaustive part. Clinical practice can be very negative. It is not easy to deal with the sick, the old, and the hurt. I desperately wanted to help people, but so many people did not want to help themselves. I felt like I cared more about my patients getting well than they did. I started to wonder if they understood the sacrifices that I was making for them.

Looking back on it, I can see that what set me apart from other successful doctor's was that I could not turn it off. My mind was in care-giving mode twenty-four hours a day. I took their problems home with me. I could help fifty people in a day. However, if one of them were not improving, he or she would be the one that kept me up at night. Helping others was destroying me.

Another mistake that I made was that I made myself too available. I wanted to be there for my patients. Most of them had my private phone numbers, and they were not afraid to use them. I would open early or stay late for needy patients. I would make house calls. I would come in on Saturdays and Sundays all too often. It was rewarding, but it stole my social life and my leisure time from me. I could not plan anything fun because I was always "on call". I had accepted this emotional predicament as the inevitable price of my success. I was telling the world that my patients were more important than my family and myself. There were more fulfilling ways that I should have been spending my time.

> "Doctors spend eight years and 200 G's going through medical school, and what do they get? A diploma on their wall and a bulls-eye on their back."
>
> - Dr. Perry Cox on the TV series *Scrubs*

The business ownership trap

The problem with being a business owner is that in order to do that one thing you love—baking cakes, practicing medicine, fixing cars—you have to do ten things that you do not enjoy. Your business is your responsibility and you have to do whatever it takes to keep it running. It is no wonder that so many business owners have tension headaches; they are wearing too many hats.

Many employees come to the conclusion that they want the easy life that they assume their bosses have. They decide to open their own business. These entrepreneurs leap into business ownership before they understand how much work is involved. They think that they can handle everything that comes with running a business, but a staggering number of them are sadly mistaken.

I wanted the freedom of self-employment, but I became a slave to it. I worked as many as 115 hours a week as a business owner. I was seeing patients eleven hours a day, and I was also the marketing department, the public relations department, and the patient education department. When I was at home, all that I could think about was work. When I was at work, all that I could think about was going home. I was in a trap that I had created for myself. I missed birthdays, anniversaries, and holiday parties. I had not been to a family reunion in five years. There is no business in the world worth that kind of time investment, no matter how sweet the paycheck. My bank account was full, but my "time account" was overdrawn. I had nice cars that I did not have time to drive. I had a beautiful house that I barely had time to sleep in. I had piles of money that I could not enjoy spending. I discovered that it was very unsatisfying to cuddle up to my checkbook or my plasma TV at night.

Unless running a business is a dream of yours that will bring passion to your life, keep your day job. Do not bring your work—or work worries—home with you unless you absolutely must. Leave your work at the office, and let your boss deal with the stress. The funny thing is that he or she probably wishes that they had the "worry-free life" that you do.

What's in a name?

In 1977, the United States Department of Agriculture dedicated its Washington cafeteria—The Alfred Packer Memorial Dining Facility—to Colorado pioneer Alfred Packer.[47] "Alfred Packer," Agriculture Secretary Robert Bargland declared, "exemplifies the spirit and fare that this agricultural department cafeteria will provide."

Several months later, the General Services Administration promptly removed the dedicatory plaque, renamed the cafeteria, and accused the Department of Agriculture of "bad taste." Packer, it was discovered, had been hung in 1874—after murdering and eating the five prospectors who had hired him to guide them along the Mormon trail into Colorado.

This story teaches two valuable lessons. First, be careful whom you choose as your tour guide. Second, a title is nothing more than a name. I am sure that the cafeteria spaghetti tastes the same whether it was named after a cannibalistic pioneer or Chef Boyardee himself.

We have become a culture where what we do has become more important than who we are. We are obsessed with status symbols and job titles, and we wear them like badges. We are constantly under attack by the question: "What do you do for a living?" Your average ice-breaking conversation may start like this: "Hi, I'm Reverend Professor Doctor Thomas Johnson, DDS Esquire." In the grand scheme of things, who really cares? What you do is not nearly as important as who you are.

My problem with titles is that they are forced upon us. They command an undue level of respect. I think that respect should be earned, not implied. We need to get over how titles make people feel more or less special than they truly are. That is something I have never understood. Why do people put professionals like doctors on such a high pedestal? I know doctors that are horrible human beings, and I know grocery store employees that I would trust with my life. Everyone is an expert at something; some things just come with fancier titles. I am a chiropractor, an occupational health consultant, an author, a professor, and a designated civil surgeon. However, ask me to fix my computer or the leak in my shower and you will see just how inept I can be. It is no accident that I have been called "the dumbest smart guy in the world" on more than one occasion.

I have always felt uncomfortable with my titles. I never once felt like I was better than my patients—or anyone else for that matter. I feel like the term doctor does not say anything about who I am; only what I do. I rarely even told people that I was a doctor, unless I was trying get out of a speeding ticket or impress a woman. I felt that my titles were for my business card and my office wall, not my personal life. I was concerned that using my titles in the wrong situation would make me seem pompous. I also feared the conversations that it would bring up. I was already giving up most of my life to my job; I did not want to talk about it when I was socializing.

I want to live in a society where we care about the type of man or woman you are instead of what you do. A society where you are more than a job title. I care about whether or not you are a good family man. I care about whether or not you are the type of person that deserves love, admiration and trust. I want to know if you are the type of person that I would want to call a friend. The answers to these questions have nothing to do with whether you are a doctor, a baker, or a candlestick maker.

I cannot think of any better examples than in my own family. My father is a veteran and a patriot, not a mail carrier. My mother is a saint, not an employee of the Nebraska American Legion Auxiliary. My brother Jack is a father who would give you the shirt off his back. He is not an electrician. My brother Rick is a softhearted animal lover, not an entrepreneur. My little brother Tanner is my hero, not a baseball player. I have been truly blessed to be a part of such an amazing group of human beings.

Money does not equal morality

We have another nasty habit as well. We think that the amount of money that a person makes has something to do with the value that they bring to this world. This could not be further from the truth. A teacher and a missionary are both much more valuable than a baseball player is—and I love the game of baseball. The only difference is that people do not pay to watch a teacher teach.

For many of us, it matters how much money people make. We equate money with importance. Our culture glorifies mega-rich celebrities. We spend millions of dollars on magazines that pay paparazzi to stalk them. We will do anything to meet, touch, or have sex with even the least famous of the celebrity class. We have an overpowering need to find someone to look up to, and celebrities are an easy target.

These people look great on TV, but when they step off the silver screen or the playing field their personal lives are often disastrous. They are great role models for talent, but terrible models for character.

Dr. Frank O'Neill

We put them on such a high pedestal that we cannot see that they are flawed human beings, just like the rest of us. These celebrities have more money than we could ever imagine, but many of them are not happy with their lives. They are really only satisfied a few days a month—on payday.

Life Lessons:

- Success is a relative term. Many people that are financially successful are unsuccessful at the game of life. Before you go after success, make sure it is really what you want.
- Would you like to be remembered for your job title and income level, or would you rather be remembered for the type of person that you are?
- Before you decide to own a business, be certain that you can handle the business owning you.
- There is a lot more to life than a high credit score. Many rich and successful people would give all of their money for the type of peace and happiness that is free.

Chapter 14

Thank God It's Monday: Finding Work that Makes You Happy

"We are at our very best, and we are happiest, when we are fully engaged in work we enjoy, on the journey toward the goal we've established for ourselves. It gives meaning to our time off and comfort to our sleep. It makes everything else in life so wonderful, so worthwhile."

-Business expert Earl Nightingale

Many white-collar executives are dangerously stressed and caught up in a rat race of deadlines, competition, and performance reviews. Meanwhile, the custodian who cleans their office whistles, smiles, and has a happy family to return home to at the end of the day. Who do you think is closer to winning the game of life?

Work represents so much of a person—the place to express yourself, learn about yourself, and develop a sense of belonging. It is a very important facet of your life. We all want to be excited about how we spend our days, and doing work that your heart is not in will make you miserable. The last thing that you want is to look back on your life and regret what you could have done but didn't. Why not try to find work that feels like play no matter how many hours you put into it?

Thank God It's Monday (TGIM)

School shootings, 9/11, global warming, and war in the Middle East. We live in a world that has forced us to step back and examine our lives. We have realized that life is too short to spend time in a career that our heart is not in. Many of us are at a point in life where we can no longer work without passion and joy. In this time of turmoil, we want to find a noble reason to get up in the morning.

When you allow your passion to guide you to your livelihood, you will be hard pressed to call it work. You will find yourself at a place where you can say: "Thank God It's Monday." Instead of counting the hours until each day ends, you will count your blessings that you have found your calling. You will have finally found the cure for the Sunday night back to work blues.

This is true of my golfing guru Dave. He gave up a great job in the insurance industry to chase his dream. He did not want to spend his days selling term life insurance. He wanted to find a way to get paid to play golf. I will never forget the happiness he felt when he picked up his first sponsorship to play on a tour in the southwest. It involved a sizeable pay cut and living out of cheap hotels, but he had never been more excited to get up in the morning.

Now is not the time to worry about what you should do. Now is the time to dream. Envision your best answer when people ask, "What do you do for a living?" Now get over your fears and make it happen.

What is the harm in taking a chance? If you try something new and fail, who cares? At least it will be out of your system. If you are already unhappy, you have nothing to lose. You have the rest of your life to regroup and do what you "should" do if things don't work out. And, just how will you feel for the rest of your life if you do not try? You will be amazed at how freeing it is to put away the safety net for a while.

"I don't paint to live, I live to paint."

-American artist Willem De Kooning

What makes work passionate and enjoyable?

Happiness comes from the nature of your work and the quality of your life away from it. Long hours at the office have no relationship to the former and take away from the latter. Every hour that you spend at your desk is an hour that you cannot spend doing the things that give life joy and meaning: quality time with your family, visiting your parents, traveling, or saving the planet.

According to a study on PersonnelToday.com, 73% of surveyed employees cited good relationships with colleagues as one of the main reasons for enjoying their work. Only 48% mentioned financial rewards.[48] Many of today's employees are turning down jobs that offer 30-40% raises. They have determined that their happiness is something that money cannot buy.

What makes people happy at work varies wildly. Some people want hustle and bustle, others want peace and quiet. Some want structure while others want freedom. Do what is right for you and yours. If you want to dig ditches, dig them. There is nothing wrong with a hard day's work for an honest day's pay. Your hands may be dirty, but your conscience will be clean.

No matter who you are, there are some underlying factors that will make you happier with your work:

1. Friendly, supportive colleagues
2. Enjoyable work
3. Good work-life balance
4. Belief that you are doing something worthwhile
5. Being part of a successful team
6. A flexible schedule

When deciding on your dream career, ask yourself how meaningful the work will be and how much happiness it will provide. The work that is the most fitting for you will use your strengths, challenge you, fit your personality, and fit into the future that you hope to create.

Before you climb the ladder of success, be certain that it is leaning against the right wall. You may be at a point in your life where you value freedom over success. Maybe you only want to work mornings so that you can be available for your children in the afternoon. Perhaps sitting down to eat dinner with your family is a priority. If so, you will want to figure these factors into your ideal career. You will need a job that gives you the freedom to create a desirable schedule.

Some of the careers that offer this kind of freedom include:

- Freelance writer
- Realtor
- Business training speaker
- Music tutor
- Caterer
- Business consultant
- Massage therapist
- Fitness instructor
- Website designer
- Online teacher

Most people think of work as work. The place where you go to do a job. Yet doing work that revolves around something that you care about can be one of the most crucial parts of having a meaningful and satisfying career. When you find the right fit, your work feels important and meaningful, you feel like you are being yourself, and you have the flexibility to do your job in a way that fits your life and your values.

> "We make a living by what we get; we make a life by what we give."
>
> -Sir Winston Churchill

You can make any job a passionate one

Before making a drastic career change, first look for passion and contentment where you are. Try to maximize the freedom in your current career, even if it is a field that is not known for it. Do your part to change the environment at your work instead of leaving or being unhappy. If that is not possible, you can leave and make a fresh start without any misgivings.

This is true of many doctors, including my mentor, Dr. Joel Pins. He has carved out a life worth living. While his peers struggle through life, he is making the most of every day. Rather than practice full-time, he decided to devote the majority of his career to education. He has found a way to get paid to travel the world. He is a keynote speaker at nutritional medicine seminars from Japan to Germany, and everywhere in between. He has a nasty habit of sending me emails from exotic locations to make me jealous. It works.

"Success is not the result of spontaneous combustion. You must set yourself on fire."

-Professional hockey player Reggie Leach

Build a career around your life

Perhaps you have to climb down the corporate ladder to find true happiness. Many high-paced executives are opting out of their high-paced lives, choosing to downshift. They have taken pride in their work, but it has kept them away from the things that they really care about.

There are more important things in life than work. Work is supposed to enhance your life; it is not supposed to control it. According to The Center for Work-Life Policy, 40% of women who return to the workforce after starting a family choose a career with lower pay and fewer responsibilities to spend more time with their families.[49] In another survey, by salary.com, 39% of respondents said that they would rather have more time off than a five thousand dollar raise.[50]

Clarify what is important in your life so that your career—or your next career—is the right fit. Visualize the perfect life, and then find a career that fits that vision. When you choose a career, ask yourself what you want your life to be like. Perhaps you want to travel, have children, or run marathons. These things are a part of how you define success for yourself. Make sure that your career will fit into that definition.

My friend in chiropractic school made the decision to value his life over his career long before we graduated. The first important decision that he made was to be smart with his money during school. He managed his expenses while his roommate—me—was blowing his student loan checks on kayaks and computer games. While most of us left school strapped with debt, he did not have to be concerned about money. He was not forced to work to keep the student loan companies off his back. His planning allowed him to choose his employment based on what was best for him and his family.

Why not try to turn your pastimes into profits. Look at what you are drawn to. Do you have a hobby or interest that you have been thinking about turning into your next career? There are examples of this all around us. There are the doctors, engineers, and rocket scientists that gave up their careers to become professional poker players. Or, the blue-collar laborers that turned their interest in home design into lucrative careers as house-flippers. Keep an open mind—the possibilities are endless.

> "What's money? A man is a success if he gets up in the morning and goes to bed at night and in between does what he wants to do."
>
> -Musician Bob Dylan

There's no place like home

Sole proprietors working out of their homes are a growing force in the marketplace. According to AllBusiness.com, revenues from these small businesses now exceed one hundred billion dollars a year. The ten million "all other" firms, which appear to be largely home-based, contribute an additional $431 billion dollars a year to the economy.[51] That is a lot of dough.

Operating a business from home offers unique advantages, including low overhead costs and the flexibility to work at home while raising a family. Such business owners make less money on average, but they see a higher return on their revenues. They earn higher net profits because of drastically lower expenses. They can afford to work fewer hours per week and fewer days per year. They are working smarter, not harder.

These business owners also save the costs associated with childcare, which can consume a large portion of the family budget. Childcare expenses in the United States vary from $325-$750 dollars a month for a child under the age of five.[52,53] These financial savings cannot be ignored.

Another benefit of a home-based business is a traffic free morning. Our major metropolitan areas are paralyzed by gridlock, with millions of people stuck on the road with better things to do. According to an ABC News poll, Americans spend eighty-seven minutes a day behind the wheel.[54] That number increases to one hundred minutes a day for commuters and parents with children at home. This "windshield" time has a major impact on our life. The same poll found that 20% of people have moved to improve their commute, 24% have changed work schedules, and 14% have changed jobs due to traffic.[55]

These traffic problems can take a serious toll. I have a friend that recently moved to Nebraska from California. Part of the reason that she decided to move to the Midwest was her two-hour commute to work. The four hours that she spent behind the wheel each day was hurting her relationship with her daughter. She found it hard to enjoy the warm weather and the sandy beaches from the driver's seat of her Hyundai.

MLM

Multi-Level Marketing (MLM), also known as Network Marketing, has changed the face of business ownership over the past few decades. There are well over ten million MLM distributors in the United States.[56] There are also millions of independent salespeople repping products such as Tupperware, lingerie, makeup, and home décor through direct sales methods. These opportunities are evolving into a large portion of the business world.

Network marketing is a brilliant concept when used properly. Emerging technologies have made it easier to work at home, while much of the stigma associated with network marketing has disappeared. It is now possible to run a home-based business from anywhere. You can work from home, in a traffic jam, or in line at the grocery store. MLM and other home-based business opportunities have developed into legitimate ways to increase your income with minimal investments of your time or money. I have met thirteen people—from Wisconsin to Mexico City—who earn more than a million dollars a year while working from home. There are legitimate opportunities out there if you do your research.

My first experience with a MLM company was a great one. It allowed me to turn one of my passions—health—into profit. I spent seven hours a week selling nutritional detoxification programs. I was helping people live a healthier life, and the company sent me a check for eight hundred dollars the first month. Within seven months, I qualified for a free trip for two to Victoria, British Columbia. Within fourteen months, I was earning two thousand dollars a month. It definitely made the walk to the mailbox an enjoyable experience.

While I had to end my affiliation with that company due to a competition clause in a business contract—legal mumbo jumbo—I strongly recommend that you look into a home-based MLM company. It is a great way to share products and services, help other people, and earn extra income. However, only consider this option if you can answer yes to the following questions:

1. Are you a high-energy people person?
2. Do you believe in what you are selling?
3. Do you have the time to spend five to ten hours a week on your business without putting a burden on your life?
4. Are you willing to take no for an answer without taking it personally?

A warning

Be certain that you do not start to see your friends and family as a sales opportunity. Remember that they are people, they have free will, and you are bringing them information to help them. Only approach them if you truly believe that it is the right thing for them. Never force anything on the people that you love. Do not torture them with manic persistence. They will not like it, you will not sell much, and your friendship will suffer.

"There is only one success – to be able to spend your life in your own way."

-American author and editor Christopher Morley

Life Lessons:

- Work is a huge part of your life. It symbolizes who you are as a person, and who you hope to become. Nobody should spend his or her life in a career that they will someday regret.
- When you allow your passions to lead you, you will find your Thank God It's Monday job. You will find the career that uses your strengths, challenges you, fits your personality, and improves your life. All that is left to do is to make it happen.
- As the percentage of Americans who are unemployed or underemployed increases, overtime hours for those who are employed steadily climb. Do whatever you can to maximize the freedom in your current career. Can you change the atmosphere at work, or will you have to move on? Only you can determine what the best step is for you.
- Perhaps you have been thinking about turning a hobby or skill into your next career. Home based businesses are an attractive opportunity that offers unique advantages. Network marketing is another great way to run a business from home. These employment alternatives can increase your income without forcing you to mortgage your future.

Chapter 15

A Job Worth Keeping: Companies That Create Passionate People

> "Real success is finding your lifework in work that you love."
>
> -American historian David McCullough

Passionate workers drive our economy, and these passionate workers are drawn to passionate workplaces. Smart companies can see how important it is to nurture the passion and creativity in their employees. Workers in these companies are satisfied with their jobs, comfortable, productive, and self-motivated. They work as a team—supporting one another. People feel extremely fortunate to be a part of these successful organizations.

Many employers make their workforce feel like cogs in the machine, while companies that foster passion and loyalty in their employees treat them like an irreplaceable piece of the puzzle. They understand the needs of their employees, and they work hard to meet those needs. The leaders are in service to those that they lead; and the companies set new standards in their industry.

We are experiencing a shift in which companies have to worry as much about their employee's emotional health and stress management as they do about their bodyweight and blood pressure.

While physical fitness and avoiding illness are critical, many other factors contribute to overall well-being. Employee health programs must address employee's ability to remain resilient in challenging times, provide tools and tips on coping with stress, help employees feel connected and engaged, and help employees see that they are making a productive contribution to the workplace.

The factors that draw employees to high-quality companies include a favorable schedule, employee flexibility and freedom, health and wellness initiatives, and positive work-life balance programs. Many of today's top employers are keeping these things in mind as they plan for the future. We no longer live in a 9-to-5 world, and employers are doing their part to adapt. According to the Society for Human Resource Management's 2005 benefits survey, 37% of companies now allow teleworking, 19% allow some sort of job-sharing program, 33% have a compressed workweek, and 56% provide flextime.[57] Employees are repaying the favor with dramatic increases in productivity.

Passionate companies also allow their employees the freedom to take chances. Microsoft Chief Technology Officer Nathan Myhrvold tells the story of an encounter he had with one of the wealthiest businessmen in the world. He sent Bill Gates a memo on a crazy idea: "I even think the title of the memo was 'a crazy idea,'" Myhrvold recalled. "And he sent me back this piece of mail that I have always cherished since then, and it said: 'This is the most bizarre, craziest idea you've ever had; please proceed.'" It is this type of trust and forward thinking that can turn a "computer geek" working out of his garage into a billionaire many times over.

The best of the best:

There are many exceptional examples of companies that are doing everything in their power to foster a happy, passionate, and productive workforce. I researched over seventy companies before I picked the following five that have set themselves apart from their competition. I chose each of them because they have separated themselves from the pack in one or more areas, including family-first initiatives, reported employee happiness, and forward thinking management strategies.

1. 3M

Whether you have heard of Minnesota Mining and Manufacturing (3M) or not, you are constantly influenced by their creations. Their ingenuity has brought us Scotch tape, lint rollers, and—most famously—Post-It Notes. These household products, along with the goods developed from their nearly six hundred patents, have turned 3M into a major player in the global marketplace. Their seventy-five thousand employees—in over three hundred locations—have led to worldwide sales of $22.9 billion dollars annually.[58]

3M is a place where employees can do their best work and achieve their full potential. Their singular commitment to make life better for people around the world makes the success of 3M possible. Their flexibility allows their employees to explore career opportunities and develop new skills without leaving the company. Their culture of innovation means that they listen to all ideas—regardless of job title or position. All of these things add up to 3M being named one of America's twenty most admired companies in 2006 by *Fortune* magazine.[59]

3M management believes that a sustainable work environment is one where the needs and concerns of the people who work there are respected and supported. In 1984, they became the first employer in the nation to offer sick-child care to American employees.[60] Employees are also able to explore a variety of alternative work arrangements, including part-time, job-share, compressed workweeks, and telecommuting. One of their newest innovations is a Work and Personal Life Resource Center that attends to the physical and emotional needs of their employees.

On a personal note, I learned a valuable lesson from 3M management while I was living in Minneapolis. I was asked to help a local university develop an occupational health program, and one of our first priorities was to tour local companies to see occupational medicine in action. While we were at the local 3M plant, I was amazed at the amount of time and money that they had invested in ergonomics and occupational health. They had realized long ago that a happy, healthy, pain-free employee is going to be more creative and productive. They were—and still are—years ahead of the curve.

2. Chick-fil-A

Truett Cathy opened the first Chick-fil-A restaurant in 1967, twenty-one years after he started in the restaurant business. After thirty-nine consecutive years of sales increases, it is now the second largest quick-service chicken restaurant chain in the United States, with more than thirteen hundred restaurants in thirty-seven states.[61]

Chick-fil-A's approach is largely driven by personal satisfaction and a sense of obligation to the community and its young people. The company has given more than $22 million dollars in scholarships to its employees since 1973.[62] When asked about this, Cathy replied, "It is when we stop doing our best work that our enthusiasm for the job wanes. We must motivate ourselves to do our very best, and by our example lead others to do their best as well." You can see how an attitude like this would be infectious to his employees.

Chick-fil-A's success is a wonderful testament to what is good about our free enterprise system. They understand that a loyal workforce is more productive than an overworked one. Cathy and his management team believe that their closed-on-Sunday policy is a crucial part of their success. Giving his employees Sunday off— for family, worship, fellowship, or rest—attracts quality employees that want to be associated with an organization that truly values a balance between work and life. It is no surprise that the chain has increased their sales every year since they opened their doors. While the business world told him he was crazy, Cathy understood that happy workers could do as much in six days as unhappy workers could do in seven.

Larry Julian, Author of *God is my CEO*, had this to say about Chick-fil-A's value based approach: "What impresses me most about Truett Cathy is that he has had the courage to follow his beliefs even though he is pressured by the world to do otherwise. Even though the business world said it did not make sense to take Sunday's off. Truett insisted on a day of rest."

3. PayPal

If you have ever bought or sold anything on the internet, there is a good chance that you have used PayPal. PayPal was founded in 1998; enjoying explosive growth that led to its purchase by eBay in 2002. It has quickly become a global leader in online payment solutions, with more than 70 million accounts worldwide.[63]

PayPal exhibits very fresh thinking about the way that they do business. Their focus on employee satisfaction has led them to more than twenty awards for excellence from the internet industry and the rest of the business community.[64] They are also on the forefront of the telework movement, which has become one of the fastest growing groups of employees in America. Teleworking—using technology to work from home—has allowed PayPal to recruit employees that value a strong family life. It gives employees more control over their schedules, permitting them to balance their work with their personal lives. It also saves each employee an average of fourteen thousand minutes per year in commute time. In addition, they have been able to learn how freeing it is to work in their underwear.

4. Union Pacific

Union Pacific (UP) is one of America's leading transportation companies. It is the largest railroad in North America, covering twenty-three states across two-thirds of the nation. Their fifty thousand employees move a tremendous amount of freight, including more than two hundred million tons of coal annually.[65]

UP is a company that is dedicated to service. This goes for employees as well as customers. They take great pride in creating a positive experience for all of the people whose lives they touch. And, this dedication has not gone unnoticed. The National Business Group on Health has honored them for their commitment and dedication to combating obesity and promoting a healthy lifestyle for its employees.[66]

Union Pacific also understands that employees need solutions to make juggling work and home easier. They have made a special effort to recruit women in a traditionally male-dominated industry. UP has repeatedly been named to the list of the "100 best companies for working mothers" by *Working Mothers* magazine.[67] The annual list honors corporations that recognize the values and needs of working families. Barbara Schaefer, senior vice-president of Human Resources for Union Pacific, said, "We are working hard to offer our employees the benefits and flexibility that will help balance work-life issues."

Some of the measures that Union Pacific offers to take care of its employees:

- "Plan Tomorrow, Today", a financial literacy campaign
- "Rest Easy", which pays half the cost of a nurse to go to an employee's home if a child or dependent is sick
- A 19,000 square foot fitness facility in its Omaha, NE headquarters. Free membership for employees, spouses, retirees, and contractors. For employees outside of Omaha, UP sponsors free membership in more than five hundred health clubs in the twenty-three state system
- A five million dollar childcare center for children from six weeks to six years of age
- Part time work with benefits, flextime, job-sharing, and telecommuting

I have multiple personal and business contacts that work for Union Pacific, and they have nothing but good things to say. One common theme that I hear from them is the tolerance and respect that UP has for their employees' values and beliefs. For instance, they allow on-site bible study and prayer meetings, and they allow their employees to pray together in their offices. They have also allowed a workplace ministry group—The Metro Marketplace Ministry (M3)—to come in prior to office hours to prayer walk the entire campus. While these programs are not allowed during work hours, and attendance is not required, the employees that take part are extremely appreciative. This appreciation shows up in the form of loyalty to the company and a better working environment.

5. Alegent Health Systems

Many employers are beginning to realize how important "thinking outside the box" is to finding and keeping an energized, passionate workforce. Alegent Health Systems is on the leading edge of this trend.

Alegent Health—sponsored by Catholic Health Initiatives and Immanuel Health Systems—is the largest not-for-profit faith based healthcare system in Nebraska and southwestern Iowa. They currently employ 8,600 employees—including 1,300 physicians—in over one hundred sites of service, including nine acute care hospitals.[68]

Recently, Alegent Health has distinguished itself as a leader in healthcare, with five-star ratings for patient satisfaction, the first Chief Innovation Officer in healthcare, and its "Right Track" accelerated decision-making process[69], which is an effort to create the next generation of healthcare.

Jarrod Johnson, Vice President of Orthopedics and Neurosurgery—and former member of the NFL Pittsburgh Steelers—is very proud of their efforts to tear down the walls of communication. They have instituted a bullpen style think tank, with overlapping job descriptions and room for creative problem-solving strategies, which creates an environment of teamwork and collaboration instead of competition and backstabbing.

Alegent is also trying to set themselves apart from other healthcare institutions by keeping the business side of healthcare from interfering with the needs of their patients. To achieve this mission, they have brought in creative, visionary leaders that are working diligently to create a culture of accountability and integrity. Their corporate integrity program holds everyone accountable and ensures that they are always doing the best thing for their patients. Included in this promise is the Community Benefit Trust, which has already provided over eight million dollars in grants to help community-based organizations that address the needs of the vulnerable and underserved.[70]

The success that Alegent has had is a glowing testament to what a company and its empowered employees can accomplish when they are working towards a shared goal. They can earn a profit without selling their soul in the process.

Life Lessons:

- Making a career choice is similar to a courtship. You are weighing the pros and cons of a relationship that could last for forty years—if not the rest of your life.
- Employees are looking for companies that see them as more than an ID number and a parking pass. Everyone wants to be satisfied with his or her work. That is why we look for jobs that make us feel like a productive part of the team. Employees also value work that allows them to take creative risks without fearing for their job.
- Employers have come to realize that they have to meet all of the needs of their employees, not just the financial ones. Great companies entice great employees with a flexible schedule, creative freedoms, health and wellness programs, and the opportunity to maintain a positive work-life balance. This allows them to build a workforce that helps them compete—and excel—in today's competitive marketplace.

Chapter 16

Conclusion:
How Does the Story End?

"Happiness is not a brilliant climax to years of grim struggle and anxiety. It is a long succession of little decisions simply to be happy in the moment."

-Author and meditation teacher
J. Donald Walters

If every journey begins with a single step, you have just taken a huge stride towards a better life. You now have all of the tools that you need to carve out a happier existence. The key is to put all of these pieces together.

The world in which we live is shaped by how we look at it. Other people's definition of you is a lot more about making them feel better. You have to define yourself. It is imperative that you keep things in perspective by questioning your motives: Is it for you? Is it for your parents? Is it for society? Only when you are able to say that you are motivated by happiness can you truly call your life your own. You will finally be at a place where you have nothing to prove to this world.

The ideas that I have incorporated into this book have made me feel appreciated at work, loved at home, and needed by my family and friends. I have emerged out of my cocoon to a richer, fuller life. I am still me, just a better version of me. The massive weight that has been lifted from my shoulders has made me feel like the sail in my life rather than the anchor. I am no longer holding myself back.

My new life is the polar opposite of my days as a workaholic. My twenty-five hour workweeks have saved me from my first one in, last to leave, lifestyle. I wake up refreshed for the first time since college. I drive to work with a smile on my face. I am truly excited about my life, and I believe in all of this for all of us. I love my life, and I wish you my happiness.

> "I define joy as a sustained sense of well-being and internal peace—a connection to what matters."
>
> -Oprah Winfrey

I cannot make it sound like it has been a pain-free transition. I have less money than I would have if I stayed with my old life. I have had to sacrifice some of the "finer" things in life. I do not live in a big house. I do not vacation in Europe. I do not drive a sports car. I may not be able to afford a four thousand dollar space-age bed, but I will sleep like a baby on my five hundred dollar mattress. I may not be able to afford another four hundred dollar blender that I rarely use. I will have to settle for a thirty dollar blender that I rarely use.

I know that I will continue to make financial sacrifices because of my decisions, but I would not change a thing. It has been a fair trade because it has given me things that money never could. Money could not buy what I was losing—my time and my sanity. You cannot put a price tag on such things.

The funny thing is that I don't feel like I have given anything up. I have simply shifted my priorities. I have learned that inner peace comes from being happy with what you have—with letting the chips fall where they may. If you are waiting to be happy until you carve out the perfect life, you will always be waiting.

Even though I am happy, I am still an addict. I have had moments when I miss my past. Workaholism is similar to any other addiction. It is a constant struggle for me to work less and play more, but I know that tapping on the brakes is the best thing that I can do. There are still times when I catch myself working too much, but those days are now the exception instead of the rule.

God has led me on an important journey to show me that he has a purpose for us all. I was living my life without a purpose until it all fell apart—showing me the error of my ways. I now feel like I have direction in my life. I no longer feel like a pinball bouncing around. I know where I have been. I know where I am. I know where I am going. I feel renewed because it took so much energy to fake my way through life.

If my writing helps one person, brings one family closer together, or saves one marriage, then it has all been worth it. If this book helps one person reach their dream, it has served its purpose. My only hope is that the person that it helps is you.

"Nothing is a waste of time if you use the experience wisely."

-Television producers
Robin Green and Mitchell Burgess

I hope that my message compels you to make continuous small strides in the right direction. Remembering what ad executive Bruce Barton said about change: "When you're through changing, you're through." The best way to make positive changes is to stay motivated and concentrate on benefits. While there will be setbacks and growing pains, remind yourself that your happiness is worth fighting for. You will see that you are doing better than you think.

We all have permission to make mistakes. Failures can be turned into lessons, waste can become investment, and negative outcomes can become exercises in responsibility. Some of your life experiences will be ecstatic, and some will be painful, but all are valuable. Never lose sight that everything is in the service of your deeper goals.

There are no guarantees that the changes you make will pay off. If creating a better life were that easy, you would not have read this book. Hospitals don't give out satisfaction guarantees with birth certificates. Nevertheless, ten years from now when you are looking back on your life, don't you want to say that you had the guts to take a chance? Besides, that is the only way to get through this crazy experience called life.

"Life is too short to wake up with regrets. So love the people who treat you right. Forget about those who don't. Believe that everything happens for a reason. If you get a second chance, grab it with both hands. If it changes your life, let it. Nobody said life would be easy. They just promised it would be worth it."

-Anonymous

Online Resource Directory
(with information from each website)

1. www.workaholics-anonymous.org

Workaholics Anonymous (W.A.) is a fellowship of individuals who share their experience, strength, and hope with each other that they may solve their common problems and help others to recover from workaholism.

The only requirement for membership is the desire to stop working compulsively. There are no dues or fees for W.A. membership; they are self-supporting through their own contributions. W.A. is not allied with any sect, denomination, politics, organization or institution; does not wish to engage in any controversy; neither endorses nor opposes any causes. Their primary purpose is to stop working compulsively and to carry the message of recovery to workaholics who still suffer.

Go to a meeting, read their literature, and practice the steps of recovery. There are over fifty W.A. meetings internationally. If there are not in-person meetings near you, share recovery internationally via phone and Internet meetings.

2. www.tvturnoff.org

The Center for Screen-Time Awareness (CSTA) is an international nonprofit organization, providing tools for people to live healthier lives in functional families and vibrant communities by taking control of the electronic media in their lives and not allowing it to control them.

Founded in 1994 as an environmental organization, CSTA has grown into an agency dealing with issues as diverse as obesity, illiteracy, violence, and the impact of electronic media on our lives. The organization is dedicated to making information available and putting you in charge of the "electronic tools" so that you can use them in ways that enhance your quality of life.

Their primary program is Universal Screen-Time Reduction; a lifestyle for the 21st Century. This program is geared towards helping people take control of the electronic gadgets in their lives. They also have a public awareness campaign called Turnoff Week. Turnoff Week is a grassroots project that works. More than one hundred organizations, including the American Medical Association, the National Education Association, and the American Academy of Pediatrics, support or endorse Turnoff Week. Since 1994, more than fifty million people have participated in Turnoff Week.

3. www.wellnesscouncil.org

The Wellness Council of the Midlands (WELCOM) mission is to lead the Midlands to optimal health through health promotion at the worksite by educating companies on the well workplace standards, recognizing companies for achievement of excellence in health promotion at the worksite, and consulting with companies and communities to develop and improve their worksite wellness programs.

The primary focus of the Council is to promote healthy lifestyle choices in the worksite in hopes that preventing disease would be more cost-effective than curing disease. The Wellness Council of the Midlands has served as model for the formation of the Wellness Council of America (WELCOA) and wellness councils across the country.

4. www.welcoa.org

The Wellness Council of America (WELCOA) was established as a national not-for-profit organization in the mid 1980's through the efforts of a number of forward-thinking business and health leaders. WELCOA has helped influence the face of workplace wellness in the U.S.

Today, WELCOA has become one of the most respected resources for workplace wellness in America. With a membership in excess of 3,200 organizations, WELCOA is dedicated to improving the health and well-being of all working Americans.

Predicated on improving the health and well-being of working Americans throughout the United States, WELCOA adheres to a steadfast set of beliefs. They believe that:

- Healthcare costs are an issue of significant concern.
- A healthy workforce is essential to America's continued growth and prosperity.
- Much of the illness in the U.S. is directly preventable.
- The workplace is an ideal setting to address health and well-being.
- That workplace wellness programs can transform corporate culture and change lives.

WELCOA produces leading-edge worksite wellness publications and health information. They also conduct training sessions that help worksite wellness practitioners create and sustain results-oriented wellness programs.

WELCOA has a variety of free resources and useful information that you can use. WELCOA has distributed more than 2.5 million articles, case studies, incentive campaigns, expert interviews, and white papers at no charge over the past five years.

5. www.worklifepolicy.org

The Center for Work-Life Policy (CWLP) undertakes research and works with employers to design, promote, and implement workplace policies that increase productivity and enhance personal/family well-being. CWLP is committed to promoting policies that enable individuals to realize their full potential across the divides of gender, race and class.

6. www.allprodad.com

All Pro Dad is Family First's innovative program helping men to become better fathers. All Pro Dad has fifty-four NFL spokesmen, multiple events with NFL teams, one thousand All Pro Dad's Day chapters, and Play of the Day daily emails that reach forty thousand fathers each day.

In addition to All Pro Dad, Family First offers iMom for mothers in every stage of parenting as well as the Family Minute with Mark Merrill, which provides encouragement for all families.

7. www.authentichappiness.sas.upenn.edu

This is the website of Dr. Martin Seligman, founder of Positive Psychology. His research has demonstrated that it is possible to be happier — to feel more satisfied, to be more engaged with life, find more meaning, have higher hopes, and probably even laugh and smile more, regardless of one's circumstances.

This site will help you develop insights into yourself and the world around you through scientifically tested questionnaires, surveys, and scales.

Authentic Happiness has almost 700,000 registered users around the world. All of the resources on this website are free.

8. www.stress.org

The American Institute of Stress is a nonprofit organization that serves as a clearinghouse for information on all stress related subjects. They maintain a constantly updated library of information and reprints on all stress-related topics culled from scientific and lay publications. Their monthly Newsletter, *Health and Stress*, reports on the latest advances in stress research and relevant health issues.

9. www.betterbudgeting.com/budgeting.htm

This site offers the free money saving tips ezine, *Living a Better Life*, which offers tons of free money-saving information as well as great resources like budgeting planners, and frugal family recipes.

Betterbudgeting.com also offers free budgeting calculator tools, free coupons, a free debt eBook, and free budgeting worksheets

10. www.elearners.com/back-to-school

A good resource for adult online learners. It offers advice on ways to keep your family involved in your return to school, the tips and tools that you will excel in the classroom, job and career development issues for online students, and tips for financing your education.

11. www.apa.org

The American Psychological Association (APA) is a scientific and professional organization that represents psychology in the United States. With 148,000 members, APA is the largest association of psychologists worldwide.

The mission of the APA is to advance the creation, communication and application of psychological knowledge to benefit society and improve people's lives.

12. www.psychologyinfo.com

Psychology Information Online provides a central place on the Internet for information about the practice of psychology. This site can be helpful to anyone interested in accurate information about the practice of psychology. They have developed the National Directory of Psychologists; a listing of licensed psychologists, sorted by state. Additionally, every State Psychological Association and State Psychology Licensing Board in the United States is listed.

13. www.psych.org

The American Psychiatric Association is a medical specialty society recognized worldwide. Its over 38,000 U.S. and international member physicians work together to ensure humane care and effective treatment for all persons with mental disorders. It is the voice and conscience of modern psychiatry. Its vision is a society that has available, accessible quality psychiatric diagnosis and treatment.

Notes:

Chapter 2

1. "Why Does Health Care Cost So Much?", by Shannon Brownlee, *AARP Magazine*, July/August 2008
2. "Calm Energy: How People Regulate Mood with Food and Exercise", by Robert E. Thayer, Ph.D., *Psychosomatic Medicine*, September 2007

Chapter 3

3. Fact sheet Compiled by TV-Free America, 1322 18th Street NW, Washington, DC 20036
4. Ibid.
5. www.medicinenet.com, "The "skinny" on popular diet plans", by Betty Kovacs, MS, RD
6. www.csun.edu, California State University Northridge website. Section titled Television and Health
7. Ibid.

Chapter 4

8. *The Physics of Baseball* (Third edition), by Dr. Robert K. Adair, Harper Paperbacks
9. The percentage is based on the number of times I saw the same issue in the time-use logs that I have analyzed up to the date this book was sent to the publisher
10. "A look under the hood of a nation on wheels", *ABC News/ Time Magazine/Washington Post* Poll: Traffic 1/31/05

Chapter 5

11. "Would You Be Happier If You Were Richer? A Focusing Illusion", by Kahneman et al., *Science,* 30 June 2006: 1908-1910

Chapter 6

12. *"How healthy are we?"*, by Orville Gilbert Brim, Carol D. Ryff, Ronald C. Kessler p. 597, University of Chicago press
13. Absoluteastronomy.com , topic discussion on midlife crisis

Chapter 7

14. Fact sheet compiled by The Center for Work and the Family, centerforworkandfamily.com
15. "Are you happy at work? Job satisfaction and work-life balance in the US and Europe", by Andrew Oswald, Professor of Economics, University of Warwick, Coventry England
16. Ibid.
17. QCtimes.com, "Discontent at work becoming the norm", Tuesday, October 28, 2003
18. The health report. Interview transcript between Norman Swan and Cary Cooper, Professor of Organizational Psychology and Health, Lancaster University, May 22, 2006
19. Microsoft Personal Productivity Challenge, survey from September 2004 through January 2005. Survey results were evaluated by ConStat Inc., an independent research analysis firm. The firm evaluated responses from 38,112 participants worldwide.
20. "Dungy Becomes first black coach to win Super Bowl", Associated press, ESPN.com, February 4, 2007
21. "NFL coaches share a legacy of burning the midnight oil", South Florida Sun, 4/14/2008
22. Wikipedia.com, Anthony Kevin "Tony" Dungy, Personal section
23. *Confessions of a Street Addict*, By James J. Cramer, Simon and Schuster
24. Workaholics-Anonymous.org homepage
25. Microsoft Personal Productivity Challenge

Chapter 8

26. "CDC: Antidepressants most prescribed drug in U.S.", by Elizabeth Cohen, CNN, July 9, 2007

27. Ibid.

Chapter 11

28. Barque4.blogspot.com, unable to find initial research, but I had the same statistics from notes of a continuing education seminar at Northwestern Health Sciences University in 2006
29. Fact sheet compiled by Western Iowa Tech Community College, Denison IA
30. Fact sheet compiled by The American association of community colleges
31. Ibid.

Chapter 12

32. "Are you happy at work? Job satisfaction and work-life balance in the US and Europe", by Andrew Oswald, Professor of Economics, University of Warwick, Coventry England
33. QCtimes.com, "Discontent at work becoming the norm", Tuesday, October 28, 2003
34. *USA Today*, 5/10/01
35. NCDA Gallup poll
36. Bureau of Labor and Statistics, Economic news release, Displaced workers summary
37. Legal Blog Watch, "Burn-out and the practice of law", blog review #86
38. "Teachers who quit", by Yaniv Nord, *Gotham Gazette*, April 7, 2003
39. "The Maslach Burnout Inventory: testing for factorial validity and invariance across elementary, intermediate and secondary teachers", Byrne B.M., *Journal of occupational and organizational psychology,*1993, vol. 66, pp. 197-212
40. WELCOA special report: "Resilience", by Larry Chapman MPH et al., 2005, welcoa.org
41. Work-life Statistics Fact sheet, Appendix D, found at http://web.wm.edu/hr/forms/Appendix%20D.pdf
42. *Sicko*, a film by Michael Moore, Dog Eat Dog Films, 2007

Chapter 13

43. The health report. Interview transcript between Norman Swan and Cary Cooper, Professor of Organizational Psychology and Health, Lancaster University, May 22, 2006
44. Ibid.
45. "Being a Happy, healthy and ethical lawyer", by Patrick J. Schiltz, *Vanderbilt Law Review*, May 1999
46. "When doctors kill themselves", by David Noonan, *Newseek*, April 28, 2008
47. *Stupid History*, by Leland Gregory, McMeel Publishing, 2007

Chapter 14

48. Personneltoday.com, "Friendly colleagues rather than money make people happy at work", by Georgina Fuller, January 8, 2007
49. U.S. Equal Opportunity Employment Commission, Meeting of May 23, 2007-Achieving Work-life balance, Horacio D. Rozanski
50. "Workers to employers: Show me the time off", by Ed Frauenheim, *CNET News*, January 11, 2005
51. Small Business Administration Office of Advocacy, Small Business Research Summary. May 2006, No. 275
52. "Child care expenses of Americas families", by Linda Giannarelli and James Barsimontov, Urban institute, 12/01/2000
53. "Child care costs", by Vanessa Rasmussen, startingadaycarecenter.com, 2004
54. "A look under the hood of a nation on wheels", *ABC News/ Time Magazine/Washington Post* poll: 1/31/05
55. Ibid.
56. "Friendshipping made easy", by John Kalench, *Harpers Magazine*, May 1, 1994

Chapter 15

57. Telework fact sheet, "Telework—good business sense!", January 22, 2007, www.CORAworks.com
58. Company information taken from 3M corporate website, 3M.com
59. Ibid.
60. Ibid.
61. Company information taken from Chick-fil-A corporate website, Chick-fil-A.com
62. Ibid.
63. Company information taken from PayPal corporate website, PayPal.com
64. Ibid.
65. Company information taken from Union Pacific corporate website, UP.com
66. Ibid.
67. Ibid.
68. Company information taken from Alegent Health Systems corporate website, Alegent.com
69. Ibid.
70. Ibid.

About the Author

Dr. Frank O'Neill has been a successful business owner, chiropractic physician, designated civil surgeon, occupational health consultant, and clinical researcher. He has worked with professional and Olympic athletes, college national champions, and the head trainer for the Toronto Raptors of the NBA. He is a renowned consultant and speaker, as well as a contributor to the Health Education and Research Foundation.

Dr. O'Neill walked away from his successful career to pursue a life that would offer him a better balance between his work and his passions. He currently works as an anatomy and physiology professor, as well as a prominent health and well-being consultant. He is the founder of the Alliance for Wellness, a speaker's bureau dealing with some of today's most pressing health issues. He has delivered more than two hundred presentations—on work-life balance, stress reduction, health improvement, and the search for happiness—for organizations in twelve states and Canada, including the Creighton University School of Medicine, John Deere, Blue Cross/Blue Shield of Nebraska, Kind and Knox, Boystown, and Briar Cliff University.

Dr. O'Neill resides in Sioux City, Iowa, where he is an active member of Riverz Edge church. He enjoys spending time with his family, mentoring young athletes, and delivering his inspirational message to any group that will listen.

Made in the USA
Middletown, DE
05 March 2018